The Salami Cutters of Washington Heights

Nelson's Kosher Delicatessen &
Restaurant

A Collection of True and Somewhat
Embellished Stories of the Family Business

Norman K. Nelson

Copyright © 2015 Norman K. Nelson

All rights reserved. This publication is protected by copyright, and permission must be obtained from the publisher prior to any prohibited reproduction, storage in a retrieval system, or transmission in any form or by any means, electronic, mechanical, photocopying, recording or likewise.

ISBN: 1516805208
ISBN-13: 978-1516805204

DEDICATION

This book is dedicated to my eldest son and business partner Steven Nelson, who recently passed away. Many of the stories in this book were wonderfully and hilariously retold by Steven to his family, relatives and friends over the years, and at all our family gatherings. I miss him greatly, and he will always be in my heart.

CONTENTS

Preface	vii
The Union Clerk	2
The Salami Cutters	6
John Doe	9
Gimme A Break	13
The Black Panthers	18
A Walk in the Park	21
For God and Country – An Embellished Account of a Mostly Imaginary Tale	24
The Wedding Party*	33
The Dumbwaiter and the List*	39
The Neighborhood	44
Bella	46
The Pritikin Diet	49
The Graduation	52
Fruit Strudel	54
The Pearl*	58
Don't Worry, Nelson*	61
You're In The Army Now, You'll Never Get Rich, Digging a Ditch, You're In The Army Now	63
The Kukhelayn	67
Barry	70
RECIPE: Norman's Noodle Pudding	74
RECIPE: Steven's Potato Latkes	75

RECIPE: Sidney's Matzo Balls	76
RECIPE: Norman's Chopped Liver	77
RECIPE: Minnie's Hungarian Goulash	78
Trapdoors & Dumbwaiters	80
The Halloween Wedding	83
The Hat-Check Girls*	87
Chicken	89
Harlem	93
Lunchtime	97
"Twenty-Five Men Turn to the Streets of Memory"*	102
"Chopped Liver Shall Runneth Over"*	104
Hi Ho, Hi Ho, It's Off To Florida We Go	106
Acknowledgements	110
About the Author	111

All stories written by Norman Nelson, except where noted with *.

PREFACE

What the hell was Nelson's? A bar? A kosher deli? A restaurant? Yes, yes, and yes! The store was conceived by my father Morris Nelson and his brother Al, who set sail from Russia at the dawn of a new century with a boatload of relatives and a dream. They all had great cooking skills, big personalities, commitment to quality, absolutely no idea how to run a business, and complete faith that they could make it a success!

The store grew up on the corner of 170th Street and Broadway, in the great city of New York. Across the street was the Uptown Theatre, two blocks from Columbia Presbyterian Hospital. On the block next to Nelson's was Perez Women's Lingerie. The rest of the block was all food. One of those businesses was Diatche's Dairy. You could actually smell their giant tubs of sweet butter. Next came Joe's Vegetables and Fruit. It smelled like an orchard. He actually let you squeeze the tomatoes. Then there was Manny's Kosher Meats, where the women chose the cuts of beautiful meats that Manny and his employees cut for them on a big chopping block.

Next was David's Kosher Bakery. The smell of fresh-baked breads and cakes was to die for. Tony's Pizza Parlor was five cents a slice, and Wang's Chinese Restaurant had a full lunch for twenty-five cents. Last but not least was Moe's Candy Store with newspapers, candy, three Root Beer Barrels for a penny, egg creams, and Mellow-Rolls; for a nickel you could buy two cigarettes from a pack of Camels. The kids played ball in the streets. There was stickball, football, and curb ball. There was marble season, pitch pennies, and Johnny-ride-a-pony, and no girls, please. But if you conversed with the group, they were all getting laid every five minutes.

So where was I? Oh yeah, OK, at Nelson's. The grill was in the window, and you could see delicious hot franks and knishes; people would drool as they stared through the glass. Every time the door opened, the smell of the hot dogs wafted out into the street and stopped you in your tracks. The hot dogs and knishes and soda were all five cents each. Those were the early days; things have changed since. Did I tell you the grill was in the window? Oh yeah, the deli was in front of the window too. Salami hung from the ceiling. A big glass case housed corned beef, pastrami, turkey, tongue, and roast beef. There was a bread-slicing machine where two-foot-long rye bread was fresh sliced.

A bar was in the back, where it went unseen. It was one of the busiest bars in uptown New York. Yet the Nelson brothers, Al and Morris, never figured out how to make a profit from it. Needless to say, the Irish bartenders did. They poured unmeasured large drinks, and if you had two, the third was on the house. The tips were wonderful; the bartenders made out great.

Meet the Nelsons: there was Morris, my dad; Al, his brother and partner; Sidney, my cousin; Minnie, the chef and Sidney's mom; me, Morris's son, Norman; and a whole lot more family members who, in one way or another, put a whole lot of time into the store. Of course we all ate for free.

In the corner of the store sat Charlie, our perpetually eighty-year-old delivery boy, whose hearing aid always needed a battery and would whistle. "Hey Charlie, we got an order for some sandwiches for the

Eye and Ear Hospital." In the back of the store stood an A&P supermarket cart that was Charlie's delivery wagon. "Hey Charlie, while you are there, see if they can give you a battery for your hearing aid. It keeps playing 'God Bless America.'" A joke, of course.

What follows is a collection of short stories and memories of Nelson's of Washington Heights, some factual, some embellished. I have written all of them down to the best of my recollection and to the best of my ability to jazz it up while telling a funny, factual story. There is no particular order—more a stream of consciousness that has been retold again and again, from generation to generation, at all our family gatherings. Please enjoy.

NORMAN K. NELSON

THE UNION CLERK

Sammy, a deli clerk the union sent over to Nelson's, walked into the store. Al Nelson, Morris's brother and business partner, asked Sammy if he knew how to work in a kosher deli. Sammy proudly proclaimed that he had been working in delis all his life and to just try him out. Al asked him if he knew how to make salads, coleslaw, potato salad, and macaroni salad. Sammy once again said to just to try him out. Somewhat satisfied, and needing an extra clerk anyway, Al sent Sammy down to the kitchen in the cellar.

New York stores have enormous cellars where they do all their preparation. We had a very large sink and a round candy stove with large burners. In the two walk-in refrigerators were stainless steel tanks for pickling corned beef. We stored all of our meats in these refrigerators: pastrami, tongue, turkeys, and hot dogs. The other refrigerators were for salads and pickles.

If you knew the philosophy of deli people of yesteryear, you'd know they believed they could fix anything themselves and didn't put any money into new equipment. Nelson's specialized in this: gum, tape, paperclips, and wires kept lights, machines, and refrigerators running. They also believed in doing everything by hand, and their equipment was medieval. All potatoes were peeled by hand (no automatic potato-peeling). Coleslaw was cut on a board with protruding blades—watch your fingers! Corned beef were cooked six at a time in a giant pot on the stove. It took two men to move the pot off the stove and to the sink where the corned beef could be cooled with water.

Norm and his cousin Sol, both in their early teens, were in the basement peeling cooked potatoes for potato salad. Although they would try to escape to play ball with the neighborhood kids, someone would find them and back to the basement they would go. A big, heavy door built into the floor of the kitchen, called a trapdoor, was the only way in and the only way out. Down the steps came Sammy the new clerk. Sammy had a red complexion, a big, round potbelly, a gleaming bald head, and an attitude of delicatessen superiority.

Sammy walked over to Norman and Solly and said he had a better way to peel potatoes. He grabbed the knife out of Norman's hand and cut himself, the blood dripping from his hand. He wrapped his hand in his apron. Morris's cure if you cut yourself was to stick your hand under very hot water and wrap it in a brown paper bag. For some reason, Sammy took that advice. "Maybe there is something to Morris's cure," Sammy said. "It stopped bleeding."

The corned beef that was on the stove was ready to come off the fire. They had to be poured into the sink filled with cold water and chilled to room temperature. Solly and Norman headed for the stove to muscle the big pot, whereupon Sammy ordered them to go back to peeling the potatoes.

Norman said, "It takes two people to get the corned beef off the stove and into the sink!" Sammy declared that it was wasted labor, and if they watched him, he would show Norman and Solly how it should be done. Sammy headed to the stove. He took off his blood-spotted apron and put one side of the apron through one handle of the giant corned beef pot and put the other side of his apron through the other handle. He then tried to lift the pot, holding on to each side of the apron. Norman and Solly stepped back in shock. Norman whispered to Sol, "This schmuck is nuts, it will never work!"

Sammy heaved the pot off the stove; so far it looked pretty good. He carefully wobbled towards the sink and realized it was much higher than he thought. With some hesitation, he began to raise the bubbling pot into the giant sink. Norman and Solly stood clear in amazement, as they watched the boiling water begin to spill down the side of the pot and into Sammy's pants. With a burning, stinging effect, the scalding water traveled south like an express train, parboiling Sammy's nuts along the way. Sammy screamed, dropped the pot on his legs, grabbed his crotch and fell to the floor in excruciating pain.

Norman and Sol took Sammy to the emergency room of the Columbia Presbyterian Hospital, left him there, and headed back to the store. Not one hour later, a voice from the kitchen called down to the cellar where Norman and Sol were once again peeling potatoes.

"I'm back," Sammy said.

"What do you mean you're back?" Norman said.

"Come on you guys, you don't think a little thing like that can deter a union clerk from finishing a day's work? It will never happen. What's next?" Norman looked at Sol. Sol looked at Norman. What could they think of next that would totally fuck up this schmuck? Such are the thoughts of thirteen-year-olds. Norman looked across the kitchen; his eyes fell upon a board with blades, the medieval coleslaw cutter.

"Not the coleslaw cutter!" Sol exclaimed.

"Why not?" Norman said. "What could happen?" Chuckle, chuckle.

The way this works is, you take a large head of cabbage and run it over the board with the blades. The blades cut the cabbage, and if you can pull your hands away in time, you save your fingers. Sol decided to go eat lunch; he couldn't watch. Norman brought out the heads of cabbage and started to set up Sammy. Whereupon Sammy told Norman that cutting cabbage was for him an every day event and that Norman need not set anything up for him; he could do it with his eyes closed.

The screams sounded like Cathy Berberian caught in a bear trap! Sol ran to the edge of the opened trap door. "Come on down, Sol, and give me a hand! We need to get this guy to the emergency room before he bleeds to death!" Norman said. Upstairs, Al got Sammy's pay ready; he was willing to pay him for the day so that Sammy need not spend a minute longer at Nelson's.

Two hours later, Sammy walked into the store; he looked like an Egyptian mummy bandaged from head to toe. He pleaded with Al to let him finish the day, but Al exclaimed that there was no way in hell he would allow him to enter the store. Sammy said he needed his clothes, which were down in the basement.

"Get your fucking clothes and get the fuck outta here!" Al said. Sammy proceeded to the trap door to the kitchen and wrestled the door open. You guessed it. As Sammy carefully descended the steps, the big trap door that he thought he had secured open started to close and whacked him on the head, landing him on his ass at the bottom of the stairs. Norman and Sol stopped peeling potatoes and looked up in disbelief. This time an ambulance was required.

As the ambulance was leaving, Al ran up and shoved the check in Sammy's hand and screamed for him to never return to Nelson's.

Later that day the phone rang, and Morris picked it up. It was Rudy from the Workers Union. "A clerk by the name of Sammy wants to sue you, Morris. I'm coming over to discuss this with you." When Rudy arrived, he ordered a pastrami sandwich and a beer. "About him suing you, we don't think he has a leg to stand on."

"That's the truth," said Morris.

THE SALAMI CUTTERS

Papa Sam was a giant of a man. He also thought he was the smartest man on earth. He was the moneyman—where the hell he got his money from nobody knows—and had no sense of humor. Manny was a gentleman, a World War II vet, and worked for the post office delivering mail on Fifth Avenue in New York. He was Papa Sam's son. Minnie and Dora were sisters of Morris. Minnie was married to another Sam, a retired tailor and poet who enjoyed his vodka. Dora, a delightful, beautiful woman, divorced her psychotic husband to marry Manny. My mom, Florrie, was a tough, opinionated lady with a fresh mouth. Morris, the owner of Nelson's, was the best chef and hardest worker of them all.

There you have the Salami Cutters, who pulled out of their asses an idea of going into the potato salad business with no real knowledge of how to do it. Papa Sam, the moneyman, claimed the position of president of the company. Manny would be in charge of the distribution. After all, thought Papa Sam, as a postal worker, Manny had great knowledge of territories. Only one problem: Manny delivered mail to just three tall buildings, and that was his only territory.

Manny would be required to deliver potato salad in his old car because there was no money to buy a new truck. Morris was in charge of production. He picked up empty cans from the bakery next to Nelson's and took them to the potato salad factory where he packed them. Manny had a friend who had a deli in Long Island. It was two hours away, but it was a start. He put two cans of potato salad in the car and took off to Long Island without any idea of how to get there. Of course Manny got lost, and it took him an additional two hours to get there, for a total of four hours!

Florrie arrived at the potato salad factory with her son, Norman, who was dressed in his beautiful white clothes. She told him to wait outside and to not get dirty. Florrie entered the potato salad factory and proceeded to tell all of them how stupid they were to try this when they had no knowledge of how to run a business. To which they all replied that she did not know what she was talking about. So the screaming went on and could be heard outside by Norman, and anyone else who cared to listen.

The phone rang and it was for Manny. His friend told him to pick up the potato salad, which had gone sour due to the long trip in Manny's car. Manny told him to just throw it out and he wouldn't be billed.

While Florrie was inside scolding Manny for the failed delivery, the neighborhood kids gathered outside, and once they saw Norman standing outside in his whites, they took a football and threw it at his head. Norman begun to scream for help, but no one inside the factory could hear him because they were screaming at each other. One kid filled a pail with mud and dumped it on Norman. Norman clenched his fists and began wildly trying to hit anything he could. It was his thought that maybe, with some luck, he could make contact with someone and maybe make them back off. Boom! He made contact. As he peeked out of his half closed eyes, he realized with a shock he had just hit the biggest, toughest head of the gang.

If he was in deep shit before, he surely was on the way to the holy grave now. This giant of a kid stepped forward, his eyes turning red. The rest of the guys stepped back to give him room. Norman had two choices. He could run down the steps to the potato salad factory and face his mom, who, God knows, would beat his ass because he got himself dirty, or he could face the gang's leader, whose eyes were red and whose fists looked liked watermelons. Norman thought to himself that this kid must eat nails for snacks. All of a sudden Norman had thoughts of grandeur. He felt like Don Quixote, whose story his teacher had read to his class. He also thought of the Jews crossing the desert eating matzo and shouting, "We shall overcome!"

The ham-fisted leader approached Norman. Norman moved in as well, ready to die for his potato salad factory and his country. The big guy kept looking bigger as he approached. At that moment, Norman thought he saw flames shooting out of the kid's eye sockets. There is no turning back now, he thought. Norman threw the first punch; the big guy caught the fist of Norman in his hand, grabbed Norman by the back, and took him to the ground. He then turned Norman face-up and sat on him.

"Hey little schmuck, you ready to give up yet?" Norman once more began to experience feelings of grandeur, remembering the story of David and Goliath. David was a little guy; Goliath was a giant. David killed Goliath with his slingshot. Norman asked himself, *Where the hell did I put the slingshot? I ain't got no slingshot! What am I nuts? This guy will kill me!*

"Hey big guy, get the fuck off of me; you're sitting on my nuts! I give up; you win!" The big guy got off Norman and dragged him to his feet.

"You want to play football with us?"

"Ok," Norman replied.

Florrie came out of the potato salad factory. All the kids could see she was very upset. The gang backed away. Florrie grabbed Norman by the back of his dirty white shirt and, with a big hand, slapped him across the backside. "Next time I tell you not to get dirty, maybe you will listen to me!"

JOHN DOE

The night was clear, crisp, and cool. You could hear the ambulances as they arrived at the Presbyterian Hospital emergency ward. But tonight the noise of the police cars took over as they arrived on the scene. The body was lying on the floor of the pavement outside the emergency ward. People gathered around to see the body. Police put up a barricade to keep the crowd away. Someone in the crowd shouted that he knew the man. The head investigator called him over.

"Do you know who this is?" he asked.

"Yes," the observer replied.

"Well who the hell is he?"

"He is Adolf Hitler!"

"Get the hell out of here, you crazy schmuck, before I arrest your ass!" the detective shouted. Other detectives arrived on the scene. "Hey, Goldberg! You ever see anything as gross as this?"

"Yeah, I seen you," Goldberg replied.

The other cops and detectives gathered around the body. Detective Sheen asked Goldberg if there was anything strange about the corpse. Detective Goldberg answered, "His eyes have been taken from his head, and his hand had no fingers; they have been cut off." Upon further investigation of the nude body lying on the cement street, Goldberg said, "They also cut off his balls, the sadistic bastard. This looks like a gangland slaying to me. What do you think, Sheen?"

"I think I missed dinner and am dying from starvation. Send a boy over to Nelson's Deli; bring back some hot dogs, knishes, and a couple of Dr. Brown's celery tonics."

Just then a Cadillac pulled up, and an older-looking gentleman with a black doctor's bag and wearing a black tuxedo came over to the men. You could see he wasn't very happy. He had just been summoned away from his granddaughter's wedding at the Waldorf Astoria. He looked at the body on the pavement and exclaimed, "What the hell happened to him?" He looked some more. "It looks to me like someone had it in for this guy. They sure as hell beat the living shit out of him."

The coroner checked the body and saw what Goldberg saw: eyes out of his head, fingers cut off, a missing ear, his testicles missing, no clothes…all on a black-and-blue, broken body.

The coroner exclaimed, "Officer, this is the worst condition I have ever seen a dead man in. It looks like it could have been a gangland slaying."

"That's what Goldberg said," replied the officer. The coroner and the cop looked at Goldberg. Goldberg looked at them , then all three looked at the body.

"Let's get you into a body bag," the coroner said to the dead man,. Turning to Goldberg, he said "Get him to the morgue. I'll check on him tomorrow. I need a drink after this."

"Yeah, me too," said Goldberg. He turned to the officer. "Get this puppy ass, whoever he is, into the morgue – stat!"

The detectives walked into Nelson's. The faces at the bar were unfamiliar. The tables were full of people who were eating Chef Mini's Hungarian goulash and having drinks. Many of the tables were taken by students celebrating their graduation from Columbia University School of Medicine. The detective and the coroner sat down by the bar. The bartender poured them their drinks, and the conversations began. Everyone wanted to know about the dead man on the pavement. Was he thrown out of a car, thrown off a roof, or what? Why was the body cut up the way it was? Was it a maniac, the Mafia, or a gangland slaying? If there was a crazy man in the community, was there enough protection? Plenty of odd stuff going on here since we brought in the homeless.

The next day the detectives were back at Nelsons. The *New York News*, the *Post*, and *Newsweek* all had front-page articles on the killing. They all pointed out that only the New York gangland could have pulled off such a killing. They finished their drinks, their sandwiches, and their hotdogs and headed back to the crime scene.

Detective Goldberg answered the phone; it was the coroner at the morgue. "Goldberg, come on over. I want to show you something strange."

When Goldberg finally arrived at the morgue, he began to peruse the dead body. The tag on the big toe of the body read "John Doe." The coroner said under no uncertain terms that this was the strangest corpse he had ever seen. Detective Goldberg continued looking over the corpse. "Where's the fucking blood? There should be blood. How come no fucking blood?"

The coroner replied, "Maybe somebody drained his fucking blood."

Goldberg replied, "What—a vampire, maybe?"

"Well, somebody or something drained his blood."

"It gets stranger and stranger," Goldberg replied, sweat coming off his fat cheeks.

The coroner went on. "Furthermore, this corpse did not die recently."

"What do you mean?"

"I think this guy was killed some time ago," the coroner replied.

"You mean a couple of days ago?"

"No, I mean a couple of weeks ago, maybe a couple of months ago. Help me turn this body over. Goldberg, you grab the legs, and I will grab the hands. When I say turn, turn him over. One, two, three, Turn!" Goldberg, with his big hands, grabbed the feet and ended up with a handful of bones.

The coroner started to scream. "Goldberg, put the fucking feet bones back on the body!"

"What? Are you crazy? I am not touching that body again!"

With the body turned over, the coroner noticed a bright yellow ribbon coming out of the ass of John Doe, playfully inviting the viewer to tug it.

"What the hell is that?" asked Detective Goldberg.

"How the hell should I know?" replied the coroner.

"Well," said Goldberg, "pull the ribbon."

"Are you crazy? There could be a bomb in there. You're the detective—you pull it!"

Goldberg mumbled something beneath his breath and began to carefully and slowly pull the yellow ribbon. Soon what looked like a piece of paper appeared. The paper up the ass of the corpse said, "Rx: If you find this body, please return it to the Columbia Presbyterian Teaching Hospital Teaching Room."

Goldberg turned to the coroner, more sweat rolling off his fat cheeks. "The press will bury us if this ever gets out."

That night, an ambulance drove up to the Columbian Presbyterian Hospital. Two men got out from the back and took out a stretcher with a body covered by a white sheet. One of the men flashed a detective's badge, told everyone to get the hell out of the way, and headed for the elevator. He got in, went to the fourth floor, and headed for the school. When he got to the students' autopsy room, he uncovered the body, sat the corpse in a chair outside the room, and then got out of the hospital as fast as his feet could carry him.

The next evening, there was a student party. Nelson's supplied the beer, salads, and sandwiches. There were balloons made up of blown-up condoms in different colors; there was also a large banner. They were welcoming back one of their own. John Doe.

GIMME A BREAK

Norman stood with his mouth open. What he saw were big yellow school buses coming in one by one. They seemed never to stop. What the hell is going on here, he thought. Goldberg has to have something to do with this. When Goldberg is involved, I get fucked.

Weeks before, Detective Goldberg had walked into Nelson's.

"Hey Norman, I have a great job for you."

"Goldberg, if you think it's a great job, do it yourself! My previous experience with you leads me to believe that anything you are giving away is a worthless piece of crap. Do me a favor, Goldberg, and give the catering job to another one of your great friends. If you suggest it, I am not touching it with a ten-foot pole. Everything I do with you turns to crap; don't try to persuade me."

Goldberg continued the conversation as if he didn't hear Norman. "Remember Alan the Jewish kid we played ball with on the block? His mother, a lovely woman, has a disease and they are not sure how much longer she will be alive. Well, she wants to see her son married before she goes to heaven. I told them you would be glad to take the job of catering the wedding."

"What do you mean you told them? What, are you crazy?"

"How can you deny a dying woman her last wishes to see her son married before she takes her last breath?" Goldberg replied.

"Goldberg, somehow anything that comes out of your mouth seems to be complete bullshit."

"Come on Norman, have you no heart?"

"No, I have no heart; I am a selfish, lying, bullshit artist, just like you! So find yourself an apron and start catering, and don't talk to me until your catering job is done."

"Please, Norman, have a heart; she is dying."

"So you say, Goldberg."

"They are willing to pay a good sum to do this job."

"What are you getting out of this, Goldberg, besides screwing me? Which seems to be the most enjoyment you get out of your lousy life."

"To tell you the truth, my nephew is the groom."

"Your nephew? You mean you have relatives?"

"Norman, take the job; I will be beholden to you for the rest of my life."

"A short life, I hope." Norman replied.

"I hate to do this to you, Norman, but the Liquor Authority is cracking down on the neighborhood bars for small infractions such as serving people that are inebriated. So far, your name is not on the list. I have been watching out for you. So you will do the catering job?"

Norman met with Jake and Freda, the parents of the bride. They seemed to have a problem talking to each other. She was a tough lady, and Jake was an alcoholic. *That bastard Goldberg has led me to the top of a mountain, and I'm about to be pushed off*, thought Norman.

"Shut your mouth, Jake," said Freda. "I will handle this. We want a wedding for around two hundred people, more or less. We want you to find a catering facility, kosher of course, with outside seating. We want tables set outside; a full buffet with chafing dishes, hot and cold; a dessert table with a wedding cake; all help, waitresses, bartenders; flowers and music, to take care of the wedding ceremony; and a chuppah."

After an hour of bargaining, they finally settled on a price. Norman was now in real shit. He had agreed to the job against his own feelings, and because of Goldberg bringing him the job, he knew that somewhere down the line he was going to get screwed. *Damn that Goldberg.*

Norman found a catering hall that was kosher with outside grounds to hold the wedding. He then went to his friends, Larry and Eileen, and asked them to set him up with a klezmer band (one that plays Jewish music in a traditional way). Norman went to Minnie and Morris and told them of the affair. They were both great chefs, and he put the food preparation in their hands.

The day of the wedding, Norman and his crew arrived at the catering hall. Minnie and Morris were inside preparing the food. Chairs, tables, chafing dishes, everything on the buffet, waiters and bartenders—all seemed to be going well. Norman had Sally the maître d' to take care of the wedding ceremony. She was to set up the procession, which would be led by the klezmer band, to the platform where she had already had some of the waiters set up the chuppah. The chuppah looked beautiful; its long white poles held up all kinds of flowers woven together to create a top.

The only problem Norman had was with Jake and Freda, the bride's parents. "Jake, you bastard, put down that drink and pay attention to the bridal ceremony. You ruin everything, Jake, you piece of crap." Jake just gazed back at his wife and smiled.

"Go fuck your self, my darling," he said.

"If you ruin this wedding Jake, I will make you sorry for the rest of your life."

"My darling, I was sorry after the first day I met you," Jake replied.

Then came the buses. All kinds of people came off those buses. They were singing and chanting. They hit the buffet table, pushed their way to the food, and swarmed around it like they hadn't eaten for weeks. *Damn Goldberg, I'm going to kill him,* thought Norman. *Where was that son of a bitch hiding?*

"Start the ceremony!" Norman cried out. That was the only way he could stop the people from finishing off the last of the food. The ceremony began, the klezmer band started playing, and the wedding party started down the aisle toward the chuppah. The rabbi was waiting for the bride and groom to approach. The groom's parents were in place at one end of the chuppah; the bride's parents were at the other end of the chuppah. At the end of the ceremony, the rabbi told the groom to kiss the bride and then step on the glass, as was the custom, which startled the bride's father, who was drunk as a skunk. He then proceeded to back into the chuppah with full force. As the chuppah began to fall, one of the four poles holding it up knocked the father of the bride off the stage and on to the ground where he lay. A voice rang out, "Is there a doctor in the house?" A man ran up.

"I'm a doctor." He looked at the bride's father. Jake had a smile on his face and started to laugh.

"You bastard, I knew you would ruin the wedding!" said Jake's wife.

Jake replied, "Screw you darling," and got up and joined the crowd that started dancing. He started to dance, and he was wonderful at it. A bunch of the men picked up Jake, sat him on a chair, raised him over their heads, and marched around to the music. Every time Jake fell out of the chair, the men caught him and put him back in the chair. They did the same thing to the bride and groom. Jake's wife was still cursing at him whenever they passed each other.

Last came the wedding cake. When it was all over, Norman thought he saw Goldberg mixing in the crowd that was heading for the buses. "Hey, Sally, were you able to take a head count?"

"How can you take a head count when the guests change tables every five minutes?" said Sally. "It looked to me like maybe you had twice the amount of people."

Jake dropped into Nelson's to pay his bill. "Jake, I counted three hundred people," said Norman.

"Are you crazy? There was no three hundred people, maybe like two hundred."

"Two hundred, are you crazy? Maybe more like four hundred!"

"Four hundred, are you nuts, maybe more like a hundred fifty! Listen, Nelson, your lucky if I don't sue your ass."

"What do you mean?"

"The chuppah fell on my head and almost killed me. If it wasn't for my wife giving me mouth to mouth, which she learned at the Red

Cross, I would be dead now."

"You're the one who caused the chuppah to fall. You were drunk, and whose fault is that?"

"The bartender kept giving me drinks after my loving wife told him not to give me any more liquor."

"I am sorry I took the job. Pay me for two hundred people and we'll call it even."

"How about a hundred ninety people and we will call it even?"

"How about a hundred ninety-five and we'll call it even?"

"How about I let you settle it with my wife?"

"OK, a hundred ninety people."

Detective Goldberg walked into the store. "Great job, Norman."

"How come, Goldberg, any time I get involved with you I end up getting screwed?"

"Norman, you are an unappreciative man. I give up on you."

Norman replied, "Thank God."

THE BLACK PANTHERS

One of those long limos stopped in front of Nelson's. Two black men got out and entered the store.

"Is Norman here?"

"Yes."

"Please let us speak to him."

Norman came out from the back of the store, changed his apron to a clean one, and walked to the front of the store. He saw two gentlemen, at least six feet tall, and introduced himself. "I'm Norman; what can I do for you?"

"Mr. Nelson, do you believe in God for all people and all races?"

"I do."

"Mr. Nelson, do you agree with the fact that all people of color are not treated with the same respect?"

"I agree."

The other man put his hand on the shoulder of the man asking the questions. "Let me take over John. Do you know who we represent, Mr. Nelson?" Norman thought to himself, the Mafia? Maybe friends of the guy he threw out of the store last week for calling him names, who said he would send his friends to kick the shit out of him? Norman looked up at these men and, feeling very unsure of himself, replied, "How the hell do I know who you are?"

"We represent the black Muslims," the man said. Norman looked outside. Two giant seven-foot-tall men got out of the car and walked toward Nelson's. Norman looked again; no one else was in sight. Where was that bastard Detective Goldberg when you needed him? They looked at Norman and asked him what the soup of the day was. They had heard that we had the best soup this side of town.

Millie, the waitress, had just arrived. When she heard that the man asked about soup, her eyes lit up. She remembered that Elias, a wealthy customer of Nelson's, had given her a fifty-dollar tip for the same soup. She quickly did her arithmetic; four times fifty equals $200. Barley and bean, the soup of the day, was brought out in big bowls. Millie sat the men down. The soup as usual was fresh and delicious.

Millie hovered over the men. "How can I help you? More soup? What can I do for you?" They all smiled, but no answer came. One man got up from the table and approached Norman.

"Norman, we are holding a meeting at the Audubon Theater three blocks from here. Malcolm X, our leader, will be our guest speaker. We will have a lot of celebrities there to speak. We know you are kosher and want you to cater the affair. We think food for one hundred people should be enough." Norman and the black Muslims arrived at a price. Norman told the men that their soup today was on the house. They thanked Norman and then left.

Millie ran to the table. In the center were a bunch of bills. She picked up the bills and started counting. All the bills were one-dollar bills, and after counting five times, she came to the conclusion that they added up to eight dollars. Millie went ballistic. She was $192 short.

Norman calmed her down, "Millie, not everyone is going to leave you a tip like Elias did. Be happy with what you get." Norman and his partner, Sidney set up trays of food for one hundred people. put it on the truck and headed to the Audubon Theater.

Upon arriving at the Audubon, Norman saw crowds of people holding signs asking for equal rights for black people. Police cars were in the area, and police were trying to control the crowds. Norman felt someone tap his shoulder. Detective Goldberg told Norman to get into the delivery truck and follow him.

Norman finally got to the back of the building where there was a delivery entrance. He and Sidney started to bring in the food. They went through a door that led to the stage where there were tables covered with cloths and paper goods. After delivering the food, Norman and Sidney headed back to the delivery truck. Being two white men in a sea of black people who were fighting for their rights felt very uncomfortable, to say the least. Norman was for equal rights, but at that time his thought was to just get out of there unharmed. He was not a hero, and neither was his partner, Sidney.

When they returned to the store, they heard the news: Malcolm X had been shot and killed

A WALK IN THE PARK

Van Courtland Park was at the end of Washington Heights, and in the center was the Cloisters, a museum made up of a scattered bunch of buildings that housed mostly artifacts from the era of King Arthur and his knights. The Cloisters sat above the park. It looked down on bike paths and gave you a great view of the surrounding neighborhoods.

A group of people walked into Nelson's at lunchtime. They ordered their lunch and asked if they could speak to Norman. Norman went to the table and greeted them. They were people he knew from the Washington Heights newspaper.

"We are running our usual medieval festival and would like you to set up a booth with food and drinks. We already have around one hundred booths and would love for you to be among them. The festival raises money for local charities, and Mr. Nelson, we have what we think is the best spot in the fair, and it happens to be the only spot still open. But we think you will do great there; it's perfect for you."

Since it was for charities in the neighborhood, Norman agreed to participate. The day of the medieval fair, Norman got together some kids in the neighborhood and packed up and headed out. Parking the truck at the fair, Norman was happy to see crowds of people arriving early. Booths were being set up on the trail that headed to the Cloisters; they were already doing early business.

People dressed in medieval attire, some on horses, and accompanied by a marching band from George Washington High School, were preparing to begin. They were assembled at the south entrance. On the way up the trail, they would march past the bike paths and would continue past a small zoo with orangutan cage and the children's small animal zoo. Eventually they would march past the north entrance to the park, and continue to the museum.

There was no short cut to get to the Cloisters. No wonder it was the only spot open. By the time you got to the top you were half dead. Norman called his group together. "Men, we have to take this hill, remember we are doing this for God and country." Some of the group told Norman to screw himself and disappeared into the crowd. The rest of the group started the haul of food and equipment up the hill. An hour later, upon passing the zoo, Norman noticed the large apes with long hands in the orangutan cage. The orangutans ran to the front, where large glass walls separated them from the onlookers. They stood on the wall, they rubbed their asses on the wall, and they screamed and stuck their tongues out. The group sped up and the Cloisters were now in sight.

Upon arriving at the Cloisters, Norman set up his grill. He had at least a hundred hotdogs and rolls, along with relishes and paper goods. He then set up his ice tea dispenser. The North Entrance to the park was just down the hill. He heard the parade and the bands approaching from the south. Down below you could see the crowd stopping at the booths on the trail and stuffing themselves with waffles, cakes, sodas, and other dishes of all kinds.

No wonder the spot was open, thought Norman; *by the time the crowd gets here they will be out of money and full.* He started grilling the hot dogs; they smelled great.

"Let's get ready troops," Norman said. The parade was about to enter the Cloisters. However, instead of marching straight past Norman's booth, they were marching to the right and leaving by the north entrance. Norman grabbed one of the medieval men dressed in armor and asked what's going on.

"We are late," he replied, and shouted out the order to proceed.

"What the hell do you mean proceed? What do I do with all these hotdogs?"

The gentleman then replied, "Shove them up your ass."

The crowd followed the parade out of the north entrance. Norman's crew picked up the equipment and the food and joined the end of the parade. As they passed the orangutan cage, Norman threw the hotdogs over the glass wall. The orangutans had never seen anything like this before. What do you do with it? Some ate them; some tried to shove them into their belly buttons; some thought they were sex items and tried to place them in other parts of their bodies.

As Norman started to follow the parade, a photographer arrived and asked if he could take his picture for the Van Courtland Park newspaper. Norman stood against the glass that separated them from the orangutans. One of them picked up a hand full of shit and threw it at the glass panel. It made a beautiful round background for the photo. A voice rang out, "Hey Norman, I always knew you were full of shit!" It sounded like Detective Goldberg.

A day later the newspaper arrived; it announced that Norman was given the Good Samaritan award for the love and compassion he had shown to the zoo animals

FOR GOD AND COUNTRY – AN EMBELLISHED ACCOUNT OF A MOSTLY IMAGINARY TALE

"What are you crazy? You want me to go undercover for you? I like you Detective Goldberg, but I am a Salami Cutter. A corned beef and pastrami man. A potato salad and coleslaw man." Norman went on. "If you need a good knish, give me a call. You need a good potato pancake, I'm your man. Goldberg, how about I make you a pastrami sandwich and forget the whole crazy idea?"

"Hear me out," said Detective Goldberg.

"Listen Goldberg, if you don't forget your stupid idea, I'm going to call the head nurse at the Presbyterian Mental Ward, whom I know personally, and she is going to come down here, put you in a jacket, and take you down to the mental ward."

"I need you," Goldberg said.

"What do you mean you need me? My wife needs me, my business partner needs me, and my kids need me. You don't know what you are saying, Goldberg; you don't need me."

"At least listen to me before you tell me to go screw myself."

"You are worse than my mother in law! OK, I will listen."

"Golda Meir, the prime minister of Israel, is coming to New York."

"So what does that mean to me?" said Norman

"She will have a party at the Top of the Fair."

"God bless her, what does that have to do with me?"

"You will be doing your country a great service," Goldberg said.

"I already did my country a great service when I was in the army for two years during the Korean War."

"I'm not talking about America; I'm talking about your true country, Israel," said Goldberg.

"What true country Goldberg? I'm American, not Israeli."

"You are the only Jew I know that fits the background I need."

"What background?" Norman said.

"You're Jewish."

"Yes."

"You're kosher."

"Yes"

"You're a chef."

"Yes."

"You fought for your country."

"Yes."

"Well your country needs you now."

"Listen, I never went overseas, I was stationed in Pittsburgh, Pennsylvania for two years and was lucky to survive that. You are making a big mistake. There's plenty of Jews around, find someone else."

"Norman I need you, I need someone who can keep me informed until the prime minister of Israel leaves New York. By the way, Norman, I also know your liquor license is up for renewal and you might have a problem applying for a new license."

"You son of bitch, Goldberg."

"So you will do it?"

"Do I have a choice?"

Norman arrived at the Top of the Fair, a building where all the parties for the World's Fair were to be held. The building looked like a ten-story-high mushroom with a heliport on top. Norman entered the elevator; the guard required his driver's license. Upon seeing the license, he said that Chef Charles was awaiting his arrival and took Norman up to the kitchen.

The kitchen was modeled after a gigantic ship's galley; it had all the latest equipment with the most modern refrigeration. The doors from the kitchen opened into a grand dining room that could seat five hundred people. This was the most beautiful dining room that Norman had ever seen. In front of the kitchen stood a glass room where the chef could view every part of the kitchen.

Goldberg had arrived earlier and was speaking with the chef. They briefly acknowledged Norman and continued conversing. Norman wasn't listening; he looked through the glass and saw about ten chefs with fancy jackets and chef's hats. They were all foreigners, mostly French. How the hell would a little Jewish guy fit in with fancy French chefs? Norman prepared himself for a good ass-kicking from the French chefs.

Goldberg introduced Norman to Chef Charles. The chef looked at Norman in disbelief. "This is the Norman you are talking about?" The way he said it made Norman feel like he would never fit in. The chef turned to Goldberg, "Where can we put him?"

Goldberg replied, "You're the chef, you figure it out."

"Not on the broiler," said Chef Charles. "I already have my staff including the best broiler chefs in France. Not on the vegetable station, not on the soup station, not on the catering."

Goldberg smiled. "Chef," he said, "How about giving him a mop and letting him clean the kitchen." Goldberg winked at the chef. Norman was no longer interested in the conversation. He was now looking for an escape route, but Goldberg's fat body blocked the door. The chef and Goldberg were hysterical. Norman was less so.

"Listen," Goldberg said, "Golda Meir will be here in two days; that's all we will need you for. We are willing to pay you $1,000 a day."

Norman said, "Take the $1,000 to the bank, change it into one-dollar bills, and shove all the bills up your ass one by one. And Goldberg, get your fat ass away from the door so I can escape you lunatics."

"Hold on, Norman. Let me show you something and if you still want to leave, you can." Goldberg asked the chef to show Norman a pile of letters. They were written by all kinds of crazies and had the dirtiest language. They all said the same thing: Death to the Jewish nation.

"What are you looking for Goldberg, are you asking me to be a moving target?"

"No."

"What then for your crazy scheme?"

"We just want you to keep your eyes open and report back to us about any unusual behavior you may see."

"What happens if I see something that gets me shot?"

"Then we will give you a medal."

"What the hell will I do with a medal?"

"I'm only kidding, nothing will happen to you."

"Do you guarantee that, Goldberg?"

"Sure."

"Just what I need, a guarantee from Detective Goldberg. Hey Goldberg, you gonna follow me around to make sure I'm safe?"

"I will always be close-by, Norman."

It was up to Norman to make sure that the kitchen was koshered for the arrival of the Israeli contingent. He needed rabbis that called themselves Mashgiachs. By the way, a Mashgiach is a jew who supervises the dietary laws (called "kashrut") of a kosher establishment. He found three houses of worship in the area. He spoke to the head rabbis, informed them that the prime minister of Israel was coming to the area, and mentioned how great it would look for them to have representatives from their temples involved.

All three temples bought the story. An hour later the three Mashgiachs arrived. They were three giant, bearded men over six feet tall with giant hands and great big smiles on their faces. They came over to Norman and started to talk in Hebrew. They hugged him and kissed him on the forehead. Norman didn't understand a word they said.

"You want we should speak English?"

"Yes," said Norman, "What are your names?" Each replied in turn.

"My name is Shamoka."

"My name is Bernstein."

"My name is Mosha. Norman we heard of your reputation." Norman looked at them in shock.

"What reputation?"

"Detective Goldberg informed us that you have given your life to help Israel survive and told us how you fought for your country in the Korean War. You are a regular war hero."

Norman thought to himself, if I ever get a hold of Goldberg I am going to kill him, the lying bastard. Just then, Norman noticed a bulge in Shamoka's side pocket. It could be a gun, he thought, or maybe it's his wallet, or maybe it is something else. Goddamn it, I'm starting to think like the picture Detective Goldberg painted for these Mashgiachs, a regular war hero.

"Let's get to work, what do you need to kosher the kitchen?"

Bernstein replied in English. "We have everything we need: just stay out of our way. It will probably take a few hours." Mosha and Bernstein went down to the truck they had arrived in and brought in machinery to wash down the kitchen in hot water from top to bottom. They then rolled out brown paper and began taking it to all the tables. All the knives and kitchen equipment were boiled in a giant soup kettle.

After taking care of the kitchen equipment the Mashgiachs moved on to the refrigerator. They took out giant prime ribs and hung them on hooks over the sink. They salted them down with kosher salt and then washed them down with water. Each prime rib was stamped with a kosher mark. The beef was then wrapped in brown paper and returned to the refrigerator. Then they proceeded to collect all the chefs' knives, forks, and other tools and took them downstairs to be buried in the ground for twenty-four hours.

Goldberg passing by Norman and stopped to look. "Why do they bury the utensils?" he asked.

"How the hell do I know" said Norman.

When the Mashgiachs were finished, they again hugged and kissed Norman on the forehead. Norman thought back to the time he was sent by his father to a Hebrew school for his bar mitzvah lessons. A bar mitzvah is when they bring a boy who is thirteen into the temple to read the Jewish bible, and he is then considered a man.

The place his father had sent him was an old temple in the midst of a Catholic neighborhood. Across from his temple was a giant Catholic church. As Norman arrived at the temple, school was letting out across the street. Norman ran into the temple before the kids from the Catholic school could get to him and give him a good ass-kicking. He ran down the steps that led to the Hebrew school. He was late as usual. The Rabbi that was in charge looked at him, slapped him on the back of the head, and in Yiddish cursed him out for being late. Norman could not wait to get the hell out of there, even though he guessed that outside, a few of the kids had probably stuck around to beat his ass.

"Nuchan," a voice said. It was Bernstein. "How do you like it?"

"Like what?" said Norman, snapped out of his daydream.

"The kitchen, schmuck."

"Oh, it's great."

Golda Meir was to arrive the next day. Detective Goldberg and his men had to be sure everything was ready for her arrival. They checked out the building, paying special attention to the stairwells that led to the kitchen, the dining room, and the heliport on the roof. They checked everything on their list and, when they agreed all was clear, proceeded to lock up and go home.

"See you in the morning, Norman," said Detective Goldberg.

"Can't wait" said Norman.

The next morning, Goldberg's men were set in place. Everyone allowed in the building had to have his name on the list. There were chefs, chef's helpers, waiters, dishwashers, pot washers, maintenance men, and police officers. It was now six o'clock in the morning, and Goldberg looked at his watch. Golda Meir would arrive in the next ten hours.

The stoves had been lit before by a Catholic man, because no Jewish person was allowed to light the stoves the night before the weekend. The three Mashgiachs were on the job—laughing, joking, and watching to see that everything was as it should be in a kosher kitchen.

Norman arrived and was welcomed by the Mashgiachs. With their big hands and laughing faces, they tossed him around like a matzo ball, hugging him and kissing him on the forehead. What the hell am I doing here? Norman thought to himself. I'm not a practicing Jew.

Goldberg walked in. "Hey Norman, how are you doing?"

"Fuck you Goldberg, go to hell," said Norman.

"Cheer up Norm, it will soon all be over." The three Mashgiachs now came over to Goldberg and hugged him and kissed him on his forehead. The chefs were cooking, and the food not only looked great, but the smells were enough to make everyone's mouth water. Only five hours to go before the arrival of the Israeli contingent.

Goldberg grabbed Norman by the arm. "Follow me."

"What—"

"Shut up and just follow."

Norman followed Goldberg, who opened the door to the ladies room. Someone had written "I will kill you Israeli bastards" across the mirror with a lipstick.

Norman looked at Goldberg. "Goldberg, I am going home."

"No you are not. No one is allowed in or out of this building until the Israeli contingent is out of here."

Norman and Goldberg went back to the kitchen. Goldberg told Norman he was not to discuss what he had just seen with anybody. The Mashgiachs upon seeing Goldberg and Norman, grabbed them and kissed them on their heads. Norman, who was on the edge of a nervous breakdown, screamed, "Enough!" The Mashgiachs had a look of shock on their faces.

"If I'm not home for dinner my wife gets very upset," Norman said to Goldberg. "You don't want to see my wife when she gets upset."

Goldberg told Norman to shut his mouth and went back into the dining room.

Shortly before the arrival of the Israelis, the lights went out. It was discovered later that wires in a ladies room electrical box had been cut. At the sound of the arriving helicopter, Goldberg ran into the kitchen. "Hey Norman, take this gun."

"Fuck you Goldberg, keep your gun and just let me go home." At that moment, the exit door to the staircase burst open, and a tall, crazy-looking man came through the doorway brandishing a German Luger. He wore army boots, lipstick, and eyeliner and had a swastika on one sleeve of his brown-colored shirt. The Mashgiachs flew at the intruder, pushed him into the exit stairwell, and slammed the door behind them, Goldberg, moving quickly to the exit, didn't make it through and hit the closed door with all his weight. The detective's gun went off, sending a bullet through his left calf. He fell to the ground screaming in pain. Norman picked up an apron and made a tourniquet around Goldberg's leg to stop the bleeding.

The door to the staircase reopened and the Mashgiachs had the tall man handcuffed. He was screaming, "Death to the Israelis." The plan had been to kill Golda Meir when she came down the stairs to enter the dining room. The idiot had picked a staircase that did not go to the heliport, where the Israelis were arriving.

The three Mashgiachs turned out to be undercover agents for Israel. They dragged the would-be assassin to the elevator and down to police custody. He was later found to be wearing a bra, panties, and women's stockings under his clothes.

Meanwhile, the ambulance had arrived; they took Goldberg to Columbia Presbyterian Hospital. When Norman visited him at the hospital, Goldberg had a big smile on his face. He was wearing a medal for bravery beyond the call of duty, which the mayor had just hung around his fat neck.

"Hey Norman, you wouldn't tell anyone how I got shot, would you, my friend?"

"No, why would I tell them what a no-good bastard you are? Listen Goldberg, before coming to the hospital I stopped at the store and picked you up some sandwiches and sodas. So stuff your fat mouth and when you get out of the hospital, come by Nelson's and we'll have lunch together."

THE WEDDING PARTY*
by Don Nelson

The wedding party was to begin in two hours. That gave me and my good friend Harry a little bit of breathing room to setup a makeshift bar in a luxury penthouse in New York City's Upper East Side. However, it wasn't nearly enough time. Let me explain.

My name is Donny. My dad, Norman owned a restaurant called Nelson's, in Washington Heights, New York. This store (we called it "the store") had been settled in that neighborhood for over sixty years, and I had to work there on weekends as a teenager. This meant that while my high school friends were going out and possibly getting laid, I was working all day and night in the restaurant. I was required to work there every other Saturday, from six thirty in the morning to ten thirty at night. Needless to say, I would have rather been anywhere else. Here was the Saturday routine:

4:30 a.m.: Get home drunk after hanging out with friends.

5:00 a.m.: Pass out in my bed.

6:00 a.m.: Wake up in fear that I had to do something—what was it? Calm back down.

6:05 a.m.: Hallucinate a large spider was crawling across the sheets. Jump out of bed freaking out.

6:15 a.m.: Pull off the sheets looking for an imaginary spider. Remember I have work. Pray in earnest that my Dad would forget I lived there.

6:20 a.m.: Try to go back to sleep. Hear footsteps coming down the hall to my room. Think to myself how could this be possible? How the hell am I going to work right now? Assume I'm in a bad dream.

6:21 a.m.: Hear the dreaded knock on my door - showtime.

I remember the earlier days. When I was younger, I wanted to visit the store. Why? Because my older brothers were forced into Saturday servitude, not me. My time was coming, but for now, I could take it easy. And when I did show up in the store, it was fun. I would play stickball with the neighborhood kids. My Dad would give me some money to go visit the old vinyl record shop next door; I would spend hours there. He would also give me the day's cash to deposit in the bank. I'd cut the long line and go straight up to the front. Who was going to stop a young, innocent child from cutting the line?

One time, I even got to bartend! You may ask if you read that right. How can a kid, still in the eighth grade, tend bar? Funny you should ask, because I asked that same question. Apparently to my Dad, anyone could bartend with the right instructions, even a thirteen-year-old.

The store was packed for lunch, as usual. "Donny, go make a whiskey sour."

"What's a whiskey sour?"

"You don't know how to make a whiskey sour?"

"No. I'm almost thirteen years old. I become a bartender when I complete my bar mitzvah, not before."

"Oh yeah? OK, well, look it up in the book."

"What book?"

"The bartender's book."

"And where do I find said book?"

"Behind the bar."

"OK. Can you help me with this?"

"We're busy as hell here; you can figure it out."

So that began my bartending career, which was over about thirty minutes later. Yes, that is correct. It took me a half hour to figure out how to make a whiskey sour. When I finally triumphed, I proudly presented the bubbly concoction to my Dad as if I was presenting an exploding volcano at a science fair. My Dad tasted it and told me my bartending services were no longer needed. Besides, the customer had already paid and left.

Which brings me back to the wedding party in New York's Upper East Side several years later. Now in my late teens, I was called up from the ranks to provide my masterful bartending skills yet again. I was in my first year of college then, so of course I had learned how to consume mass quantities of alcohol. However, I still didn't know how to make a whiskey sour or any other drink, for that matter.

I asked my friend Harry to work as a waiter for this wedding party. Now, my friend Harry was a great guy and a hard worker. However, Harry liked to drink, and a drunk Harry was a funny Harry. But a funny Harry could easily turn into an obnoxious Harry. Obnoxious Harry could create all sorts of trouble—usually for the person who made the mistake of confronting him. But deep down, Harry had a great heart, and he was a loyal friend.

My older brother Bobby was the headwaiter at this gig. He claimed to know more about bartending than I did, but if you can recall the earlier part of this story, I was the one with "professional" experience. Besides, I could always ask Bobby questions if I needed help. Plus, I had the trusty bartender's handbook. Only one thing was missing. I needed to test my drinks before I unloaded them on these unsuspecting partygoers, most of whom were doctors from Columbia Presbyterian Hospital. We had an hour left before show time. Now, who could I possibly find at this short notice to judge my mixology skills? Hmmm...

"Hey, Harry, could you come here for a sec?"

"Yeah. What's up?"

"I just made this margarita. Can you try it and tell me what you think?" Harry tastes it.

"Sure...seems OK...might need some more sour mix, though."

"Cool! Thanks, Harry."

So, back to mixing I went, in order to perfect my creations. I wanted to get it right, which meant creating another drink from scratch. As Harry went back to setting up, my original creation went with him, and he proceeded to consume it in less than three seconds. I hadn't noticed. I was too busy getting another one set up for testing.

Two minutes later:

"Harry—think this is one is better?" Harry walked over.

"Not bad…better than the other one. What else you got?"

"Uh, let me think…"

"How about a White Russian?"

"Yeah, I could do that!"

"Cool. I'll be back."

Thirty minutes and ten drink experiments later, Harry is nowhere to be found, and the party is just getting started. I hadn't noticed. I was focused and feeling pretty good about my technique. My first order came from a nice distinguished-looking older gentleman with a bow tie. "Hello, young man. I would like a screwdriver please."

"Hi. Uh…great…yes…just one second…uh…" I spotted Bobby.

"Hey Bobby, quick question."

"Yeah?"

"How do you make a screwdriver?"

"You don't know how to make a screwdriver?" Bobby walked away shaking his head and laughing.

"Young man, you don't know how to make a screwdriver?" the distinguished gentleman asked.

"Not really. I never made one before. Could you tell me what's in it? Wait—I have a book that will tell me how…just one sec while I look this up…"

"Young man, just pour some vodka and orange juice into a glass—half and half—it's that simple."

"Oh, OK, got it. Thanks, I really appreciate it. You see I'm not really a bartender. I go to Buffalo University and I'm…" The man sighed and looked bemused, with one eye on me and the other eye on the vodka bottle, as I told him my life story. Meanwhile, the number of guests waiting for drinks started to resemble a conga line. I was only a quarter of the way into lecturing the man on Descartes and other fine philosophers I had just learned about in PHI 101, when Bobby stopped by and told me to get my head out of my ass and move it along. I gave the man his drink and thanked him, mentioning I would love to tell him more about it later. He smiled politely at me, grabbed his drink, and floated over to his group in a daze, as if he had just avoided a pileup on the freeway.

As I was starting to get the hang of this thing they call bartending, the line of thirsty guests finally started moving. Most guests were asking for wine, which was a piece of cake. Every once in a while, I was thrown by some exotic drink request, like a blue mumu or a sloe gin fizz, but I already had a system to handle that. As soon as I had some downtime, I would mix the new drink and call in my reliable tester Harry, to see how well I did. Where is Harry, by the way? I thought to myself. "I don't know any Harry," a handsome woman politely reflected back to me. Apparently, my inner monologue was out.

"Oh sorry, I'm looking for one of the waiters...can I get you something?"

"I saw one of your waiters go into the second bathroom—haven't seen him since. I have to tell you he seemed pretty toasted."

"Oh, boy. Excuse me for one minute, please." I ran to the second bathroom, fearing the worst. When I got there, my fears were confirmed. In the bathroom were ten completely drained cups of my best experiments. The window was fully open, and no Harry. I started to panic. I looked out the open window down into the street, and I saw a crowd had formed around our delivery van, directly beneath the window, twenty stories below! "Holy Shit!" I said, and ran out the servants' entrance in the back of the apartment. I ran down twenty flights of stairs, burst open the back door of the building, and almost fell out on to the sidewalk. The crowd was fairly large and the police had arrived. I fought my way through the onlookers to see what they could see and finally got though to the front. In the delivery van, with the doors wide open, head hanging out of the van, was Harry, passed out from ten experimental drinks and two of the largest joints one can smoke in a penthouse bathroom.

THE DUMBWAITER AND THE LIST*
by Robert Nelson

Every other Saturday at two o'clock after the lunch rush died down, the manager Bernie, a.k.a. the Beanstalker, because of his thin build and height, would create a list of stock needing to be brought up from the downstairs basement, a.k.a. the dungeon. Beanstalker would prepare his list literally by eye, opening and closing the glass and then the metal refrigerated cabinets with the deft skill of a maestro composing a symphony. Each cabinet had its own distinct sound, with the swift slamming of one door accompanying the opening of another in a syncopated rhythm, like a percussion section in the Philharmonic - a regular Leonard Bernstein of the delicatessen world was he. Within minutes, the list was created and passed to me, and then it was off to the kitchen for my journey down to the dungeon.

The dungeon door literally was a trapdoor that opened underneath the feet of Frank, the dishwasher. Frank was a great guy, always a smile on his face and a song in his voice. "Don't let nothing take a bite out of you down there," he would say as I descended the grease-covered steps into the pit of despair and heard the dungeon door slam shut behind me with a loud thud. The light switch was at the bottom of the stairs, so I would be in total darkness till I got to the bottom and searched by feel for the switch. A little about the light switch and my dad's business partner Sidney. When something broke, Sidney would patch things together with a can opener for a screwdriver and a bungess as tape. A crack in a window—stuff a piece of bungess in it. An electrical wire frays—wrap it with some bungess. Cut your finger—make a Band-Aid from bungess. You get the picture. So Sidney fixed the frayed and busted light switch with a can opener, screwdriver and some bungess, and this is how it stayed repaired for years. There was a good reason why Sidney's hair stood on end. While doing electrical fixes he would electrocute himself, and I guess over the years he built up some level of tolerance to it, but the electrocutions gave his hair a permanent.

Now that you have some background, I can get back to the story. If you got to the bottom of the stairs standing upright, you passed your first test. The next test was groping by hand for the light switch like a blind squirrel. Well, every now and then even a blind squirrel will find a nut, and I would eventually find the light switch. The key was to reach for the dried bungess and follow due east for ten inches till I reached the switch. But be careful. If I turned the switch without simultaneously removing my hand from the toggle, I would experience a jolt from an electric shock. Having mastered the technique through trial and painful error, the second test was passed. Now where had I put that list?

Surprisingly enough, there was order in the way the basement dungeon was laid out. The paper goods room was on the left. The first of two giant walk-in refrigerated boxes was dead center. This box housed the meats. To the right of the walk-in box was the cabbage shredder, a.k.a. chicken fingers because of its propensity for cutting one or more of your fingers if you let them get too close to the always-exposed cutting blades. Walk further south and I'd grope for light switch number two. I could find the switch easily enough but, through the marvel of "Sidtricity," I had to shimmy the bungess-covered wire to the switch in order to turn it on—always with a spark, so we affectionately called this switch Sparky. With Sparky on, I could see the second walk-in box and the soda and beer storage areas. The second walk-in box held the pickles, the coleslaw, and the potato salads. My brothers and I thought there might have been a dead body or two in there, too. The back area was also home to the dumbwaiter that is the topic of this story, so let me get started.

A dumbwaiter is a metal three-foot-high by three-foot-wide box that is raised and lowered by a hand-crank-driven chain. While cranking to the right, it transported all of the stuff in the dungeon to the counter upstairs, where the Beanstalker was waiting to unload. Of course the dumbwaiter was falling apart and had to be held together with the usual deli supplies, but the lock that held the dumbwaiter box in position had not worked since the 1940s. A thick piece of metal, which most likely came from an old oven door, was shoved into the hand crank at just the right time to keep the dumbwaiter box in a locked position.

It took a good hour to get all the supplies, as the Beanstalker never put like items together—that would have been too convenient. Once the dumbwaiter was filled to capacity and the hand crank turned to drive the deliverables upward, I would have to hold the crank in one hand and deftly maneuver the oven door handle to lock the box in place. A plastic button in the middle of a metal circle would then be pressed—carefully, so as not to touch the metal, or I would get another shock—and it would sound a buzzer upstairs, signaling for the box to be unloaded. The hard work was to load and to crank, but the Beanstalker would take his sweet-ass time unloading, which made my time in the dungeon that much longer. A slam of the upstairs dumbwaiter door and a buzz signaled the box was now empty and ready to be refilled – pull the metal handle and crank to the left to bring it down.

A sequence of fill-crank-buzz-shock-wait, repeated four or five times, and the list was done. But every time without fail, just as I was about to make my way out, the buzzer would sound. This time was no different. Buzzzzzzzzzzzzz.

Lights that had been turned off were now turned back on, and over to the dumbwaiter I went. Buzz back up…the door opens. "Blah blah blah blah blah soda."

"I can't hear you!" I screamed up.

The Beanstalker put his head into the dumbwaiter box and screamed, "Send up a case of cream soda," then slammed the door shut.

I loaded the case of cream soda, cranked up, insert metal rod, buzzed, shut lights, and started to make my way out. Buzzzzzz. What now? Lights back on and buzz back.

"What?"

"Blah blah blah pickles."

"I can't hear you!"

Beanstalker, with head in the box, yelled out, "I forgot—send me up a can of sour pickles."

Getting pickles sucked! I had to go into walk-in box number two, where the interior light did not ever work, and, in the faint light coming through the open door, plunge my arm into the brackish, briny waters of a five-foot-high pickle barrel to fish out the fifty or so pickles needed to fill the pickle bucket. The process took some time, as I could never scoop up more than five pickles with each plunge. Making matters worse was that the only freaking thing that worked properly with that walk-in box was the auto-close feature on the door. I had to truly be a contortionist to keep one foot holding the door open while balancing precariously on the other foot, which stood on the petrified carcasses of pickles that had been brought forth from the briny depths but failed to make it to freedom. If the door closed on me, which it often did, I was locked in the dark walk-in box searching for the push bar door release and praying it would work, lest I become like the petrified pickles. Ten up-to-the-elbow-dives and the bucket was filled, and my whole now-pickled arm stunk like the sea. All the neighborhood cats would follow me home!

Pickles now on the dumbwaiter, it was time for crank-buzz-shock-wait, listen for the dumbwaiter door to open, listen for pickles being pulled out, and listen for dumbwaiter door closing. OK, lights off, and I made my way toward the stairs leading me out to freedom. Buzz buzz buzzzzzz. Oh shit, what the freak now? Lights, shock, and a slow march back to the dumbwaiter. Buzz buzz. "OK, what now?"

"Blah blah blah napkins."

"What?"

The Beanstalker dips his head into the box and yells, "I need a case of napkins and another salami."

"Why the hell couldn't you put this all on the list the first time?"

Let me tell you a little more about the Beanstalker. He stood about six foot two and was a fairly skinny guy, thus the name Beanstalker. He looked especially like a beanstalk because he was topped off with a lopsided toupee that looked like a piece of overgrown vegetation or a dead koala bear. The Beanstalker thought no one knew about his toupee, but you would have had to be blind not to notice.

But back to the story. It was then, as I was contemplating sending up a box of TNT, that an idea struck me while scaling the racks looking for that last box of napkins. I headed back to the dumbwaiter. Buzz buzz. I hear the door open. Beanstalker said, "Yeah, what? The box is still up here and it's empty. When are you going to send up the napkins and salami?"

"The box is stuck," I yelled.

"What?"

"The box is stuck."

But it really wasn't. The Beanstalker's head was still in the box as I removed the oven door handle and turned the hand crank. The box immediately started its descent and just caught the Beanstalker as he instinctively pulled his head from the moving box. I heard a scream of pain and a lot of cursing as the box descended to the basement level. I smiled in satisfaction, as I had exacted my revenge. And my prize? I caught me a Beanstalker, and his stanky-ass veggie toupee was now sitting in the dumbwaiter box down in the basement dungeon with me.

THE NEIGHBORHOOD

Morris Nelson was the original Nelson of Nelson's. He opened Nelson's on the corner of 170th Street. Morris started as a clerk on the same street that Nelson's was on. Morris contacted his brother, Al, who had done well in the printing business. If Al was willing, Morris would split the cost of a new store on the corner.

In those days landlords gave long-term leases with a clause to repeat the lease with a raise in the rent of about 10 percent. After some haggling, Morris and Al took a lease. They told the landlord they needed six months to start up the business. At that time the news coming out of Europe was not good; the landlord was thrilled to start a new lease and gave Morris six months free rent.

Tuesday was Morris's day off, and he had hired a checkered cab belonging to Sam Cline. Sam was having his usual lunch, a pastrami sandwich and a Dr. Brown's cream soda. Morris, Florrie and their son Norman arrived at Nelson's. Florrie and Morris were not talking to each other as usual, because Morris had the audacity to mention his brother's name in the presence of Florrie. Big mistake. Maybe not really such a big mistake, because this way Morris would not have to converse with Florrie.

Sam finished his meal. "Ready, Morris?" The Nelson's entered the cab. The cab took off and headed to Radio City Music Hall. At that time Radio City Music Hall charged an exorbitant amount of money: four dollars for adults and two dollars for children.

Morris stopped the cab a block from the theater as he usually did. He entered Lofts knowing exactly what he wanted. The Clerk handed him a box of the most delicious candy you could ever eat. They were nuggets surrounded by nuts and covered in chocolate. The box had eight pralines—one for Norman, one for Florrie, and the rest to be enjoyed by Morris.

At that time Radio City Music Hall featured the news, a cartoon, the main feature, and a full stage show. After the show, the family went to the upstairs Chinese restaurant. Ninety-five cents for lunch, two dollars for dinner. After leaving the restaurant, they met Sam who was waiting with his cab.

"Hey Norman, want to go to a party?" One of the girls in the neighborhood was having a party. The guys as usual were talking about getting in her pants. When they arrived at the party they found out that the girl had planned it without her parents knowing. All the guys, who by the way were all virgins, talked like guys who were laid at least three or four times a week. The girls approached the guys; the guys approached the girls; then the door to the apartment flew open and the girl's parents entered. The guys took off and ran down the stairs. A few blew their load as they got to the street. The next day the conversation was about how everyone was laid at least five times.

Norman thought to himself, where was I? How come everyone was getting laid within five minutes of arriving? It would probably take me five minutes to get my pants off.

"How did you do Norman?"

"Pretty good."

"How many times?"

"At least eight times."

"You are kidding Norman! You hold the world's record!"

"When we go to the next party I'll double my record!"

BELLA

The trolley stopped in the center of the street across from Nelson's. It was jammed with people heading to uptown New York. The open-air buses headed up and down Broadway. You could see the entire crowd and the stores. What a great ride. The Eighth Avenue subway headed down Broadway, a very fast way to travel downtown. When he had his choice, Norman loved to ride the trolley or the open-air bus. And so another day began.

Norman opened the store and heard that the nurses at Columbia Presbyterian had gone on strike. They picketed at steps of the main entrance to the Hospital. Norman knew them as his customers.

"Hey Charlie, lets serve them coffee and Danish," Norman said.

"OK, I'll get my delivery cart ready," said Charlie. By the way, Charlie's delivery cart was pilfered from the A&P supermarket across the street.

Norman arrived at the steps where the nurses were on strike, set up a table, and began serving coffee and Danish. Some of the top executives came out of the hospital.

"Hey Nelson, get the hell off the steps before we have you arrested for trespassing," one of the executives said. The answer came from the nurses.

"You touch a hair on his head and you will see the biggest riot you have ever seen." The police started to approach. Norman got hold of Charlie by the collar.

"Charlie, let's get the hell out of here before they kill us." Charlie grabbed his A&P cart and followed Norman down the steps. "Hey Charlie, don't worry about picking up anything, let's just get the hell out of here." Charlie followed Norman, his hearing aid playing "God Save the King."

Norman opened up the store and the telephone rang. "This is the Democratic Party of Washington Heights. As you know, being a true democrat"—Norman thought to himself, First I get involved in a strike, then I get involved in politics—"Bella is having a rally, and it will be coming down Broadway with a parade. She will be on a large stage being pulled by a car. We need to feed her."

"Ok," Norman said.

"She only eats kosher."

"So."

"We want you to get her a chicken dinner. She won't be able to stop."

Norman hung up.

Norman heard the parade that Bella was in coming down Broadway. After the big buildup about being an important part of the Democratic Party, Norman felt he had to do his part. He took a hot chicken off the counter, wrapped it in paper and put it in a brown bag. Since he wasn't getting paid for this, he wondered if he could write it off his taxes as a donation to the Democratic Party. Norman ran down the block to catch up with Bella who was on a platform covered with flags and balloons. She wore her big trim hat as usual. The platform had stopped at a light at an intersection. Norman knew he had to get the chicken to her before the platform and Bella began to move again. He shouted to one of Bella's aides who was riding on the platform, wound up and threw the brown bag with the hot chicken with all his might.

His aim seemed to be pretty good, however the brown bag came off the chicken; then the wrapping paper flew off; then the chicken seemed to come alive with wings flapping as it headed for Bella. Norman stood there with his mouth open. The bird flew on and arriving at the platform hit Bella in the chest. The crowd turned to Norman and accused him of trying to blow up Bella with a bomb in the shape of a chicken. Norman saw some blue uniforms running toward him. The crowd started to yell, "Get the bastard! He tried to kill Bella!" Norman pushed through them and headed for the back door of Nelson's. He hid in the basement for an hour.

THE PRITIKIN DIET

Norman woke up with a strange feeling like he was floating in the sky. He opened one eye; the sky was blue with clouds. He opened the second eye—more sky. Was he dead? Had God taken him to the beyond? He heard a carol in the background, "Come ye Christian soldiers..." What the hell was going on? Norman turned his head; there were bars all around him. God had finally caught up with him. Norman raised his head. The George Washington Bridge came into view. He realized he was sleeping on the fire escape.

What a schmuck, he felt himself saying. Come ye Christian soldiers? I'm not even Christian. Norman dressed and headed for the store. He had a luncheon and a coffee break to cater at Columbia Presbyterian Auditorium. It was the largest auditorium in New York. When he arrived with the delivery truck, he proceeded to set up coffee and Danish for two hundred people then went back to the store to prepare a luncheon for Dr. Pritikin, who was having a discussion on how to stay healthy by eating healthy foods.

Don't use any salt, sugar, spices, or cream. Norman thought to himself, are you kidding me? Who the hell could eat food like that? Norman began to prepare chicken and fish—no meat, please. He also prepared salads and vegetables of all kinds and desserts—but no sugar, please. Are they nuts? Norman tasted the chicken. "Ach! This is terrible." Norman added a little salt, a little pepper, duck sauce, soy sauce, garlic, Chinese fish sauce, ketchup, tomato sauce, and onions. *Now this has got a taste*, Norman thought to himself.

He did the same for the fish, sautéing it in cream, butter, salt, pepper, garlic, chopped pepper, and onions. Next, he prepared fresh salads with delicious oil, vinegar, salt, pepper and dressings. *Don't forget the hot homemade rolls*, he told himself. For dessert, there was Morris's famous fruit strudel and coffee.

Everything was set up and ready to go at Columbia Presbyterian Auditorium. Norman told Bernie the clerk to watch the buffet. "Don't let anyone near it until I get back." Norman left to pick up some last-minute food.

A short time later, a guy walked through the front door of the auditorium and headed for the buffet table. His shirt was messed and up sticking out of his pants. He was wearing black and white sneakers. Bernie approached him. "Can I help you?"

"I'd like to taste the food, please."

"Are you crazy? No one gets near this table. Who the hell are you?"

"I'm Pritikin."

"You are who?"

"You heard me; I am Pritikin."

"If you are Pritikin, I am the president of the United States." Bernie grabbed him by the collar and pushed him into the street.

Norman returned to the auditorium to open the buffet. People began to pour out of the auditorium and started to devour the food. They had never tasted diet food so good in all their lives. They all wanted Pritikin to give them the recipe. What was his secret? The police came in the back door holding the man that Bernie had thrown out earlier. The man kept shouting, "I'm Pritikin, I'm Pritikin!"

Upon seeing this man, Norman said, "Mr. Pritikin, good to see you."

"Thank God it's you Norman, your idiot clerk kept throwing me out."

"Mr. Pritikin, I'm sorry. Have some food."

Everyone seemed to be having a wonderful time eating the beautifully prepared food. They all came over to shake Pritikin's hand. Mr. Pritikin smiled. The food was delicious. He asked Norman what the secret was to preparing such delicious food. Norman answered, "Mr. Pritikin, Nelson's cannot give out its food preparation secrets."

THE GRADUATION

The neighborhood has changed since I grew up in it. When I grew up it was mostly Jewish and Christian mixed. As the years went on, those people moved mostly to Long Island, and Hispanic people moved in. The kids growing up in the neighborhood played mostly the same games. They respected their neighborhood and were good friends to Nelson's, which they respected as one of the better restaurants. It was part of their neighborhood.

When Norman received the news that the Columbia graduating class wanted food, he sent out a message in the neighborhood that he wanted ten kids to help with the party. He then called the company that delivered all the meat products to Nelson's.

"Hey Dan I need a favor. I need you to help me deliver a large order to Columbia University with your truck."

"Are you kidding?" said Dan.

"Do I sound like I'm kidding?"

"I have business to take care of."

"I'm not asking you to give up your business; I just need a favor. I am one of your best customers, right?"

"You are," said Dan.

"I pay on time, right?"

"You do."

"You are going to help me deliver the order, right?"

"Right."

Next, Norman called Atlantic Bakery. "Is Sam there?"

"Yeah."

"Hey, Sam this is Norm at Nelson's. I need a favor, Sam."

"What do you need?"

"I need fifteen six-foot Italian breads with fifteen wood boards six feet long to be delivered to Nelson's."

"It's done."

The night before the party, Norman and Steven begin to slice up enough meat to fill up all the bread. Then they prepped Russian dressing, lettuce, tomato, pepper, and mustard. When Nelson's closed that day, twenty kids showed up.

"Hey, we've got too many kids," said Steven.

Norman said, "Don't worry Steven; just add it to the payroll. We're not turning anyone away.

That night, they lined up the kids. One put on the corned beef, one the pastrami, one the turkey, and so on for the lettuce, tomato, pickles, and Russian dressing. They chilled a couple of cases of Coke and made a bunch of sandwiches for the kids to eat. Everything moved like a well-oiled assembly line, with lots of jokes and lots of singing. It was a thing of beauty.

That next morning after paying the kids, Norman and Steven piled the kids into their jeeps and drove across the Washington Bridge to a diner in Jersey. When they returned to the store the meat truck was waiting. Steven and the kids took charge of the packing and delivery of the party.

FRUIT STRUDEL

Morris, my father, was an exceptionally smart man except when it came to business. He came from Russia. Don't say that in front of Florrie, his wife, who thought she was much superior because she was American. Although my father and I were never close, I did feel a great respect for him and in later years felt sorry for not being closer.

On the other hand there was my mother Florrie. I believe she was two different people at the same time. Whenever she came into the store, she changed into the devil. For some reason she always picked on the clerk. "Change your apron you slob; wash your hands. What the hell are we paying for. Morris, how can you put up with this jerk; you are throwing out your money." However, when she went to the register and spoke to the customers, they all fell in love with her.

My father was always teasing me, and I hated it. He never let up and made terrible comments about me. Later, when my son Steven became my partner, I found myself behaving like my father. Please forgive me, Steven. It's funny how we become our parents. I believe many people have had close to the same experience. Everyone can tell a story. Enough, it's time to get down to my real story: Morris's Secret Cocktail Strudel Recipe, which I will not disclose out of respect for my dad.

The store was jammed with people from the Columbia Presbyterian Hospital: nurses, doctors, secretaries, and more. Customers also came from different parts of the neighborhood. Sitting at one table were two well-dressed gentlemen. They finished their meal and ordered two servings of Morris's fruit strudel. They both agreed it was one of the best desserts that they had ever eaten. After they had their strudel, they came to the counter. "Morris, you got a few minutes?"

"Not really but I will accommodate you." The three men went back to the table and sat down.

"We are interested in your fruit cocktail strudel."

"It's $4.95 a pound. How much would you like?" Morris said.

"Morris, we are interested in buying the recipe and giving you a percentage of what we make. The name of our company is ———."

When Morris heard the name of the company his eyes lit up. It was one of the most prestigious companies in the frozen packing field and was in every supermarket in the country. Norman, who heard the conversation, found himself repeating under his breath, "Make the deal, please God, make the deal."

Morris looked up at the gentleman and said, "You must understand this is my personal recipe. No one will ever get it. I will produce it myself. I don't need anyone to steal it from me."

The two men looked at Morris in shock. Norman who gasped for breath, also looked at Morris in shock. Morris returned to the counter, a big smile on his face. Norman returned to the counter ready to throw up. That day Morris told Norman of his plans to go into the strudel business. The Salami Cutters had struck once more. The idea was 100 percent good. The business sense was 0 percent good. Norman felt as if he was going down the rabbit hole but, out of respect for his father, listened to the plan. He, Morris, would make the delicious ingredients that went into the fruit strudel. He would then make up the dough that formed the crust around the strudel. He would then pack pans with two pounds of strudel and put the tops on.

Norman said to Morris, "What do you mean put the tops on; you need a machine to put the tops on, and you need a label."

"Listen, Norman, we are not spending any money on a fancy machine. You take a spoon and push down around the edge, pushing the rim down while holding the top to the tin." Norman looked at

Morris.

"You are kidding."

"You know I don't have to do this; I'm doing this for you," Morris said.

"Really? You're doing it for me? How about you don't do it for me and we forget about this whole thing. Maybe we can find the guys who made you the offer."

"OK, Norman, if you don't want to be a part of this, maybe I can find someone to be my partner."

"OK, I'll do it." Norman could hear the toilet in the background as he went down the drain.

The next day when Norman arrived at the store, he could smell the fruit strudel Morris had spent the whole night preparing. Morris was totally committed and expected the same from all. Norman and Marty, Norman's brother in law, packed and weighed the tins. Time to put the covers on by hand, which was an impossible task. Without a machine it was hard to make the tops fit.

Morris said, "Goodnight; I am going home. I did my part. It is up to you to finish."

After two hours of trying to fit the covers to the tins, they had two cases of twelve tins each. Marty turned to Norman. "This is a disaster!" Norman agreed.

"What do we do now?" he said. "We have to sell this stuff."

"That's up to you Norman; I did my part. I'm leaving. Good luck."

"What do you mean, good luck?" Norman looked around and found himself alone.

He put the cases of strudel in his jeep and made stops at different supermarkets. Once in the market, Norman asked to speak to the manager. Either they were not in or they didn't do the buying. Of course, no market had any freezer space as that was at a premium. At the last stop, the small neighborhood market, Norman was able to speak to the manager.

"It will cost you a one-hundred-dollar bill to get your product in here."

"OK."

"The policy is we don't pay for the product until the end of the month, and because it is a new product, we have the right to return the product if it does not sell."

Two weeks later, Norman got a call to pick up the strudel. All the covers had come off and were sitting in the back of the store. Norman never picked up the strudel. How the hell had he even gotten into this mess? I remember, he thought. The Salami Cutters had pulled him in. He now had the right to call himself a true and valiant member of the Salami Cutters Clan. How lucky can you get? Some people never make it.

THE PEARL*
by Robert Nelson

It was my twelfth birthday and to celebrate my dad Norman said, "Why not come to work in the store?" He had just become partners with his cousin Sidney in the store on 170th Street and Broadway in Washington Heights, New York. I thought it would be cool to see the store and the city, so Dad didn't have to ask me twice. Off we went on our way to the store in what later became known as the Deli Mobile.

We arrived and Sid said, "Hey Norm, we just got a catering job for a wedding in Harlem for noon today, and you'll have to make the delivery. I already started to make the platters. Aren't they beautiful?" As wise and as nice as Sidney was, he was a much better creator of stories than he was creator of deli platters, and Dad took over to show everyone how it should be done.

Well, within the hour we were packed in the Deli Mobile and on our way to the 125th Street YMCA where the party was to take place. As we headed south on Broadway, the neighborhood started to change, and the further we went, the more it changed. At twelve years old, I really had not seen Harlem or its people. It was July 8, 1972, and we were in the midst of a New York heat wave. Fresh out of the race riots and protests of the 1960s, I thought that Harlem was a pretty scary place to be for a twelve-year-old white boy from Queens. We pulled into a spot by an open fire hydrant whose water supply seemed to have just run out. Dad said, "Wait here with the car while

I go get some people to help us bring the food in." So I waited outside, a little white boy in a dirty white apron, standing on the corner of 125th Street and St. Nicholas Avenue on one of the hottest days of the year, guarding a car full of food without a friendly face in sight. I was attracting the kinds of hard stares from passersby that you only see in movies just before a gun or a knife comes out.

It seemed like an eternity, but Dad finally came out with the minister and five members of the congregation, all of them eager to help bring the food inside. Dad unloaded the Deli Mobile and handed me the cardboard soda boxes that held all the platters of food. Just moving made you sweat, and moving fast to unload these platters had everyone sweating pretty good that day.

At one point, I looked up and could not believe my eyes as I saw something that resembled a six-foot-high wall of water with a black head popping out the top of it coming our way—and it was moving fast. The minister must have seen my frightened look and said, "Don't worry son, that just be Pearl. She's the mother of the bride." All six foot two and three hundred fifty pounds of her was stuffed into a big blue dress bounding up the block on a collision course with me. I stood behind the minister as he said, "Pearl, these fine young gentlemen bring the food for the party."

In a voice that was so sweet and so meek, Pearl says, "Thank you boys. I came to help." At this point there was only one box left, and as I peered into the Deli Mobile, I could see that the box was very wet. Sidney had made the coleslaw platters and had not drain the coleslaw well, so lots of the coleslaw juice leaked out and soaked the cardboard box. Now I may have only been twelve, but when I looked at that soaked box and I looked at my dad's concerned face, I knew trouble had come a-knockin'. Like a game of hot potato, Dad snatched up the soaking box and unloaded it quick into my hands. Following his lead, I quickly unloaded it into the waiting arms of Pearl. It seemed that things happened in slow motion after that, as the bottom of the box let loose. Like a balloon filled with water, the coleslaw platters now sped quickly toward the street and exploded in all directions with a cascade of coleslaw juice that rivaled the fountains of Rome. I ducked behind the minister to keep from getting hit. After what seemed like an eternity, the spray of slaw and juice finally cleared. I looked up, only to see Pearl in her shiny blue dress covered in wet colseslaw. It took another couple of seconds until Pearl let out a scream that is still traveling today through the furthest regions of deep space. I never knew the word shit could sound like sssssssshhhhhiiiiiiiiiiiiiiiiiiiiiiiiiiit!

I pretty much thought my life was over. I could not move. I could not think. I could not blink. Dad said, "Quick, I already got paid. Let's get out of here before there's a riot." We jumped into the Deli Mobile and sped back to the store.

DON'T WORRY, NELSON*
by Robert Nelson

We had a late night catering job to deliver. "Hey Charlie," Norman said to our ninety-year-old delivery boy, "I got a delivery for you but your going to need another person to help." Charlie was as deaf as a piece of wood and just as dense, with a hearing aid that seemed to play "The Stars and Stripes Forever."

"Ok Norman, I'll get my friend Carlos to come help," Charlie said. Charlie went out for a few minutes and came back with Carlos, who was stinking drunk. Carlos tried to stand up straight in the doorway.

"Hey Charlie, I think your friend Carlos here is a drunk," Norman said. Charlie gets offended.

"Your wrong Norman. Carlos ain't no punk. He's a good man."

Norman yelled in Charlie's ear. "I said drunk, not punk!"

Carlos heard this and said, "I no drunk Nelson. You no worry. No worry Nelson, no worry."

Against his better judgment, Norman said, "OK."

Charlie and Carlos started through the door, platters in hand. Charlie's hearing aid started playing "The Stars and Stripes Forever," and Carlos sang "No worry Nelson." Not more than two steps out the door, Carlos spun around and dropped both meat platters on the ground, yelled "Holy shit, man," and ran off down the street.

NORMAN K. NELSON

YOU'RE IN THE ARMY NOW, YOU'LL NEVER GET RICH, DIGGING A DITCH, YOU'RE IN THE ARMY NOW

Sunday was the day that Norman dragged his sons from their beds, put them in the jeep, and headed for the Washington Heights store. Norman felt they should learn how hard it was to earn a living. They thought about running away from home and hiding out in the woods to escape.

In the rear of the store stood an old fashioned phone booth; many times people would call the store using that number. The phone booth rang. Norman went to answer it, pulled open the door to the phone booth, and saw Donny inside asleep on the floor. Norman had been looking for him for the past hour. Donny ran out of the booth, and Norman answered the phone.

"This is Dolly." Dolly was a beautiful black woman who spent a lot of money at Nelson's. She only ate kosher food and loved Nelson's.

"Is that you, Norman?"

"It's me."

"My daughter is getting married."

"Congratulations!"

"I've decided to do the wedding party. I need you to do the catering."

"Sounds good."

"It's going to be about two hundred people."

"When do you need the party?"

"Tonight."

Norman sat on the phone for what seemed like minutes. "Did you say tonight?"

"I know it's short notice."

"I would have to be a magician to cater a wedding party on such short notice."

"Money is no problem."

"Ok, I'll do it."

Dolly said she would provide everything herself, all she needed was the food.

"Where should we deliver the food?"

"In Brooklyn," Dolly said.

Norman had no idea where Brooklyn was. As far as he was concerned, it was another world. He lined up the troops: Bobby, Steve and Donny. When he told them about the job they were going to, they looked at him in disbelief. "Only a true Salami Cutter would take a job like that," Norman said.

When Minnie walked into the store, Norman told her to put up two large briskets, three corned beefs and her favorite cherry sauce, four pastramis, and four tongues. Norman would put up three large turkeys and make his noodle pudding, a giant Caesar salad, and any side dishes he could think of. He'd also take care of the potato salad, coleslaw, and pickles.

The troops disbanded and started on the jobs they were given. Sidney came in to give him a hand. All kinds of delicious foods were coming out of all corners of the store. The war was on. Around six o'clock the food was ready to be loaded on the two jeeps. Each jeep had a radio that they could use to talk to each other. Norman, whose sense of direction was lousy, had no idea how to get to Brooklyn, so he told Steve he would follow him. Steve said that they should keep in touch on the radio telephone. Time was disappearing, so they packed the jeeps and set out for Brooklyn.

Norman called Steve on the radio. Bobby, who was in the jeep with Norman, had come up with a song to the tune of KC and the Sunshine Band's "I'm Your Boogie Man" that he sang to Steven and Donny: "I'm your deli man, that's who I am; I'm here to give you whatever I can—pastrami, salami, and corned beef." Fifteen minutes later came a reply from Steven: "I'm your deli man; I'm your deli man; kosher treats. I'm your deli man; I'm your deli man; come taste my meats."

Back and forth they went for an hour and a half while Nelson's of Washington Heights searched Brooklyn to find Dolly's party. They finally found a building with the number Dolly had given them. Norman went into the building to find out where the party was and saw no one was around; this didn't look good. As Norman was leaving the building, a moving truck pulled up, and it's crew started moving tables, chairs, flowers, and all kinds of stuff into the building. Norman went back to the jeep and told everyone to follow the procession into the building.

Following the movers, they were led into the cellar of the giant building. There was a twelve-piece band warming up. Dolly came in and said, "Hey Norman, thanks!"

"No problem, Dolly."

"Hey guys, set up the buffet table first thing." The table had a pink cloth and a pink skirt. Big bowls of roses were put on the table. Tables around the room were set with pink cloths, roses as centerpieces, beautiful dishes, and silverware. A six-tier wedding cake was next to the band. Dolly came over to Norman and hugged and kissed him, thrilled with the way it had turned out. After bringing in all the food, Norman and his crew left and headed for the jeeps. They had met the challenge and won the war.

On the way back to the store, Bobby sang, "I want to cook for you; I want to clean for you; I want to be your deli man, hey hey." Then Norman joined in.

"You guys have left me in awe; you are the best deli men that I ever saw."

Dolly came into the store the next day with a big smile. "Norman that was the best wedding I have ever seen! The food was sensational. How much?"

THE KUKHELAYN

This story is about my early childhood around the age of ten, as I remember it. In the summer months in New York City, the weather gets very hot, and as a young New Yorker, I was among those who tried to figure out how we could avoid the heat. One way for the kids was to go camping. We got together, my friends and me, and headed up to the roof.

Some of the guys brought food, and I, of course, brought a three-foot-long salami that I took from Nelson's refrigerator when no one was looking. The rest of the guys brought juices, fruits, and bread. George Platus was given the job of chef, so he brought a giant tub to make the soup. He set up the giant tub on cans of sterno, and added chicken stock, seasonings, chicken, and vegetables. Just when the water started boiling, the door to the roof opened, and there stood a giant woman screaming at poor George.

"George, I'll kill you, you little bastard! You know that when I come home from work I need my giant tub to soak my feet." When the kids heard that, they all started for the roof door and ran down the stairs screaming, "Ahh-ahh-ahh!"

So what does this little tale have to do with my story? Nothing, but it helps to show the weather conditions in the city during summer. Upstate New York was filled with communities where the women, leaving behind the hot streets of New York, came to spend their summer in bungalows with a central kitchen—the Kukhelayn—where they could cook their meals. They played mahjong and poker all day long. The kids were left on their own to go discovering and play on the grounds. In the evenings, the teenage kids headed for hotels: Grossinger's, Nevele, Concord, Nemerson. The subject of the day for the teenagers was how to sneak into hotels that didn't want outside visitors.

Florrie went to her favorite outside vegetable stand to shop. She saw a sign at the stand that pointed to a hotel on top of a hill. She decided to inquire at the vegetable stand, did they think she could rent the hotel for a week? She spoke to the owner of the vegetable stand, who gave her the address of the hotel owner. He and Florrie made a deal. All she had to do now was get everyone together for a fun vacation.

When Morris came to visit Florrie for the weekend, Florrie told him to close up the store for a week's vacation. They were taking everyone to a hotel that she had just discovered, the Swan Lake. Morris was stunned, but as usual, Florrie made all the major decisions. A week later they started arriving at the hotel. Minnie, Morris, Dora, Manny, Papa Sam, Grandma Ray, around twelve kids, Al, Mary, Sidney and Jerry with their wives, and other people I didn't know. I never found out who they were.

Cars kept pulling up to the hotel, and people kept getting out, carrying all kinds of uncooked foods. Minnie, Dora, and Morris went straight to the kitchen. It was big and had a wood-burning stove. Morris declared, "We need wood!" Norman and Solly had brought their Boy Scout axes and started chopping. In about an hour they had plenty of wood for the stove.

"I will do the baking!" said Morris.

"Since when do you bake?" said Minnie.

"I will bake you out of the kitchen!" said Morris

"Those words are war!" Minnie said.

The fight was on. The kitchen became a bakery. Out came all kinds of spices, all kinds of preserves, nuts, jellies, raisins, and a few things that I couldn't identify. The smells of the fresh baked pies and breads drove us crazy. People came out of the woodwork to come see the bakery and eat all the baked goods that they could chew down.

While the baking was going on Dora prepared her brisket, baked potatoes, and a beautiful vegetable dish. The cooking went on for a long time. Solly kept cutting wood while Minnie, Morris, and Dora kept cooking breakfast, lunch, and dinner, and the guests kept eating.

Besides cutting the wood and picking fresh berries, the boys did all the entertaining by telling dirty jokes. Norman: "There once was man from Alcatraz whose balls were made out of brass; he clanged them together and played stormy weather, while lightning shot out of his ass."

Solly: "A man was sitting on the railroad track eating his latkes. Along came a railroad train and hit him in the tchotchkes." Norman and Solly fell down in hysterical laughter.

The Salami Cutters got together and decided maybe they should buy the hotel. Thank God that never worked out. It would have been the potato salad factory all over again.

BARRY

Don't get me wrong, in many ways Barry was special. He would give you the shirt off his back if asked. He never turned anyone down. He also had a personality that could sometimes drive you crazy. I am his uncle, so I am taking the chance that he won't have it in for me for this chapter on him. I love you Barry, please forgive me.

My brother-in-law Marty ran the Nelson's Deli that was in Great Neck, Long Island. It was a great little store on the wrong side of the street, with parking privileges across the street at the Great Neck shopping center. Most of Marty's family worked at the store: David, Ritchie, and Barry. The rowdy ruckus and arguments went on daily. If you didn't come for the food, you came to see them argue over everything and anything. Barry, the middle child, was the loudest and nastiest. Marty was on the brink of a nervous breakdown. He decided to call the Washington Heights store and see if he could talk them into taking Barry to work with them.

The phone rang at Nelson's. "Hello?"

"Hi, Sidney. Is Norman there?"

"Yes he is, I'll put him on."

"Hi, Norm; this is Marty."

"Hi, Marty. What's new?"

"Not much. I'm calling you for a favor. You know the kids who work for me, including my son Barry?"

"Yes."

"We have all come to the conclusion that we will work better if we can get Barry to leave."

"Ok."

"Could you use him in your store? He is a terrific worker."

"Let me ask my partner. Hey Sid, we've been busy lately. Could we use another deli clerk?"

"Whatever you think."

"Hey, Marty? Send Barry here, and we will try to fit him in."

Barry arrived the next day two hours late and parked his car outside by the fire hydrant—always good for a ticket. Barry came into the store, put on an apron, and started to talk about the terrific, terrible traffic jam. It took him forever to get here. He nearly had an accident. He cursed out a lady driver who came out of her car to punch Barry out for using dirty language to describe her. She had a bat in her hand. Barry quickly scooted past her and on he went.

His first customer was a lady who came in each day for her chicken.

"I'm Barry, what can I do for you?"

"I need a chicken." The chickens were piled up on the counter, warm from the oven. Barry picked up a chicken, "This one's a beauty."

The lady said, "I don't like what it looks like."

"What are you blind? It's a beauty, lady."

"I want a different one, the one you chose looks like crap."

"What do you mean it looks like crap? You must be blind. You need glasses, lady."

"Give me the one on the bottom," the lady said.

"What are you nuts? You want me to give you the one on the bottom?"

"Yes."

"It will never happen. I'm not giving you the chicken from the bottom."

With that the lady walked out the door. Barry screamed after her, "Don't ever come back!" Sidney and Norman looked at each other in shock. They sent Barry down the stairs to the basement to send up beer, soda, and other supplies. If he wasn't around customers he was OK.

Sid and Norman knew that they had to get rid of Barry. He had been with them a week and was worse than ever. By that time, he had twenty parking tickets and really didn't want to make the trip from Long Island to New York.

In his conversations with employees he admitted that he hated the store, the employees, the customers, and the cops who gave him two or three tickets every day. Sidney couldn't take it anymore.

"You hired him Norman. He's your family; you get rid of him," Sidney said. Getting Barry back to the Great Neck store would not be easy. However, Norman devised a plan. The next time Marty called to find out how Barry was doing, Norman got on the phone.

"Hey, Marty. How you doing?"

"I'm OK. How is Barry?"

"Marty, thank you for allowing Barry to work for us. He is a wonderful kid; he would give you the shirt off his back."

"Is he working behind the counter waiting on customers?" said Marty.

"Barry has a wonderful personality."

"He does?"

"Marty, the customers are all in love with him."

"They are?"

"Our sales have gone up since he has been here."

"No kidding? What's the secret?"

"Respect. Just a little respect. Pat him on the back and he is great."

"I appreciate all the effort you put in to training him, but I think he belongs back with his family," said Marty.

"It's going to be hard to give him up. We have all become

accustomed to his personality and the great way he talks to the customers. But since it's about family, we will break it to him that he is going back."

"Hey Barry, I know it's going to break your heart but your father wants you back in Great Neck." While Norman was still talking, Barry headed out the door, got in his car with the brand new tickets on it conveniently parked at the fire hydrant, and sped away.

A week later, the phone rang.

"Norman, Marty's on the phone."

"Hey, Marty. How's Barry doing?"

"Are you kidding? He is twice as bad as when I sent him to you. How about you take him back because he was so wonderful working for you?"

"Not a chance in hell," Norman said and hung up.

RECIPE: NORMAN'S NOODLE PUDDING

Ingredients:

2 boxes egg noodles

2 cans fruit salad

4 eggs

1/2 lb. sweet butter, melted

2 pt. sour cream

2 pt. cottage cheese

3/4 cup sugar

Directions:

Boil egg noodles until soft. Dump the hot water out of the pan, keeping the noodles hot. Add butter and mix with the noodles. Add sour cream, cottage cheese, and sugar to the warm noodles, also adding fruit salad, juice included. Beat the eggs, and add to the noodles, mixing fast so the eggs don't cook. Pour in pan or dish and put in the oven until brown and bubbling.

RECIPE: STEVEN'S POTATO LATKES

Ingredients:

4 large potatoes

2 oz. flour

2 tbsp. chopped onions

2 eggs

1 tbsp. cooking oil

Small bunch chopped parsley

Directions:

Peel potatoes and soak for one hour. Drain and grate the potatoes. Add beaten eggs, sifted flour, parsley, and salt and pepper to taste. Put in the refrigerator for one hour. Add oil to a frying pan. Make sure it is hot and bubbling. Use a large soup spoon to add the mixture to the hot oil. Brown on both sides and remove from pan. Put on napkins to absorb the oil.

RECIPE: SIDNEY'S MATZO BALLS

Ingredients:

4 oz. matzo meal

1/2 pt. of boiling water or chicken stock

1 tsp. finely chopped parsley

1 egg

1 tbsp. of oil

Dash of baking powder

Salt and pepper to taste

Directions:

Pour boiling water or stock over matzo meal and mix well. Add beaten egg, oil, salt, and pepper. Put in a bowl and refrigerate for one hour. Remove from the refrigerator and roll into two-inch balls. Put into boiling water or chicken stock for fifteen minutes.

RECIPE: NORMAN'S CHOPPED LIVER

Let's put it this way, right; this ain't your mama's chopped liver. For this recipe you can use either chicken or beef liver.

Ingredients:

2 lb. liver

2 chopped onions

6 hard-boiled eggs

2 large rolls or French bread soaked in chicken stock

Salt and pepper to taste

Directions:

Cut up liver into one-inch pieces and cook for 5 minutes in boiling water with the eggs. (The eggs should be cooked with the liver and then shelled.) Fry onions in oil until brown, positively not burned. Burning the onions will change the taste. Squeeze out chicken stock from rolls. If you have a chopper, add all the ingredients and chop until it comes together in a thick paste.

RECIPE: MINNIE'S HUNGARIAN GOULASH

During the early years of Nelson's, in Washington Heights, there was no air conditioning, no television, and on a hot summer night people walked the street to get fresh air. Some of them stopped at Nelson's to have a drink at the bar and a bowl of Minnie's Hungarian goulash, which was the only available item at that time of night.

Ingredients:

4lb. cubed beef

6 sliced carrots

4 cubed potatoes

3 tbsp. extra virgin olive oil

5 cups thinly sliced onions (4 large onions)

4 tbsp. sugar

4 minced garlic cloves

2 tbsp. sweet paprika

1 tsp. spicy paprika

2 bay leaves

4 tbsp. tomato paste

2 tbsp. balsamic vinegar

5 cups chicken stock

1/2 cup tomato ketchup

2 tsp. flour

Directions:

In a large sauté pan, heat the olive oil and sauté the onions and sugar until caramelized. Add garlic and cook a few minutes. Add sweet and spicy paprika together with bay leaves. Sauté another five minutes until fragrant. Add tomato paste and ketchup. Deglaze with vinegar. Add stock and pieces of beef shank, salt and pepper to taste. Bring to a boil, then lower to a simmer and cook until beef is tender, about one-and-a-half hours, stirring occasionally. After one hour, add all vegetables and flour. Taste and adjust seasoning with salt and pepper.

TRAPDOORS & DUMBWAITERS

To tell this story I have to introduce my cousin Jerry, a good-looking, college-educated ex-GI of the Second World War. Jerry, as a lieutenant in the army, was given the job of entering towns and getting information so that the American troops could then enter the towns with fewer casualties. During those four years in the army, Jerry experienced the tragedies of war up close: desperate people blown up in their homes, people displaced, and of course, concentration camps. His hate for the Nazis knew no bounds.

When Jerry returned to the states after serving his country, he ended up living with his parents Minnie and Sam and spent a lot of his time hanging around Nelson's. Norman, a teenager at that time, looked up to Jerry as a war hero and a ladies man, and by the way, one of the best dancers Norman had ever seen. Whenever there was a family party, a bar mitzvah, or a wedding, Jerry would impress Norman with his dancing ability.

Now let's talk about trapdoors and dumbwaiters. The early restaurants had doors built into the floor that would open to staircases leading to the basement, where most of the food production and storage took place. At Nelson's, one trapdoor was behind the counter in the front of the store; the other was in the kitchen below a big sink for washing dishes, pots, and pans. Behind the counter was a dumbwaiter. This was was a box that could be lowered to the basement, and products could be loaded into them and sent up to the deli counter. In Nelson's, the dumbwaiter had broken down after years of heavy use. If you cranked it up to the deli, it would come right back down to the basement.

Morris devised a solution where, if you shoved a pipe into the chain-drive wheel that moved the dumbwaiter and let it dig into the wall, it would hold the dumbwaiter in place.

"How about having someone come in and actually fix the dumbwaiter so it actually works the way it should?" Norman said.

"Forget it; why pay to have it fixed when you can have your own cure," said Morris.

Whereas Nelson's never put a penny into new equipment, when it came to food they always had the best. The coffee was great too. As usual, the coffee man came into the store making his weekly delivery of the best coffee you could purchase at the time. Carl, the coffee guy, who had a thick German accent, told everyone he had arrived and would put the coffee away over the sink in the kitchen.

Jerry happened to be in the store, and when he heard the German with the thick accent, he went berserk and started screaming at him. "You lousy Hitler-loving German bastard!"

In reply, Carl shouted, "You Jew bastard! The Arian nation will take care of you and your kind!" That's all that Jerry had to hear; he went wild at that point. Sidney, Jerry's brother, grabbed him, sat him down, and called for the bartender to bring him a shot of whiskey. At this time, Carl the coffee man, with his bags full of coffee, was strutting through the store. To get even with Jerry he started to sing the German national anthem. Jerry watched with his eyes bulging, "I will get that Nazi bastard if it's the last thing that I do!"

Carl proceeded to the kitchen and as he always did, climbed the sink to stack bags of coffee onto the shelves above. After filling the shelves with coffee, still singing, Carl jumped off the sink. You could hear the German national anthem get lower in tone as Carl disappeared into the basement with a crash like two cymbals in a marching band. Someone had opened the trapdoor under the sink. Jerry ran into the kitchen, looked into the basement where Carl was getting to his feet, and called out to Carl, "You lousy Nazi bastard," whereupon Carl, refusing to give Jerry the satisfaction, started to climb the stairs still singing the German national anthem. When Carl was just about to enter the kitchen, the trapdoor closed hitting Carl in the head and causing him to fall back down the stairs. Jerry opened up the trapdoor again and once again, Carl was singing his way up the stairs.

Jerry took off through the back delivery door - we didn't see him for a week. When Carl was finally out of the basement, he indignantly marched over to the counter and bellowed that he would not be delivering coffee anymore; the Jew bastards could go to hell before he would allow them to have his special coffee. He marched back to the kitchen to grab his wagon, then carted himself out of the store singing the German national anthem.

THE HALLOWEEN WEDDING

The phone rang, "Is Norman there?"

"Yes."

"Tell him it's Sam from the Second Avenue Deli." Norman took the phone.

"Hello?"

"Hey Norman, it's Sam from the Second Avenue Deli."

"OK."

"I need you to do me a favor."

"OK."

"This couple asked me to do a wedding for them."

"OK."

"You know, Norman, I don't do weddings. Your name came up when I asked my customers if they have ever used a caterer. They loved your work. Will you do the wedding?"

"OK."

The next thing was to meet the bride and groom. The address was a giant building on the East Side of Manhattan. As Norman entered the apartment, he was very impressed with the beautiful decorations. A middle-aged, white-haired man greeted him. "I'm Bill. Nice to meet you, Mr. Nelson," he said.

"Just call me Norm."

"As you can see, Norm, I'm not a youngster and neither is my wife-to-be. In my case it's my third marriage, in her case it's her second. We want a wedding that our friends will never forget."

"What kind of wedding?" said Norman.

"We will have a regular temple service, but the celebration has to be exciting and unusual," said Bill. "I have taken the top floor party room for the affair; it has a refrigerator, bar, stove and anything else you need."

Norman asked him again what kind of wedding he had in mind.

"Well, since it is the week of Halloween, we want a Halloween wedding. We want it to be youthful, with a Halloween theme."

Norman thought, no wonder Sam from the Second Avenue Deli didn't want to do the affair. But, that didn't stop Norman; it was exactly the kind of thing he loved to do. (He had a true Salami Cutters attitude: Jump first and think later.)

Bill went on, "It's all in your capable hands; don't let me down."

"How about the wedding cake?" said Norman.

"A four- or five-tier cake with all kinds of Halloween decorations. A Halloween table built up to the ceiling with Halloween candy, masks, horns, and anything else you can think of."

"Sounds great so far!"

"We will need a full bar. I will supply all of the booze, and you supply the rest of the bar."

"Sounds great, Bill. The food and the staff will be supplied by me. Hatcheck, waiters, bartender, decorations, cake, fruit table, and dessert table."

Bill thanked him and Norman left. Norman got in his car and headed for Great Neck, Long Island, where another Nelson's Restaurant resides, owned and operated by Norman's brother in-law. He went directly to Benkert's, one of the great bakeries. When the owner, a friend of Norm, heard about the Halloween wedding cake, he looked at Norm in disbelief.

"It will be expensive."

"No problem," said Norm.

Norman corralled the staff. Steven, Bobby, and Donny, his three sons who had been working with him in his store and, on occasion doing various catering jobs. All had catering savvy, were good looking, and full of fun. The hatcheck girls were Elaine, Norman's wife, and the next-door neighbor, Edie (pronounced "eedy"), who was practically family. When Edie and Elaine got together, they were a lot of fun. Norman knew they would greet the guests and make them feel at home.

Norm and his caravan of delivery trucks arrived at the East Side building, and the crew went into the lobby where they were greeted by a good-looking man who was about six feet tall and two hundred pounds.

"Can I help you?"

"Yes, we are the caterers for the Goldberg's wedding party."

"What wedding party?"

"The Goldberg's wedding party."

"I was never informed of a wedding party."

"Well, call them and ask them." The good-looking man dialed the phone.

"No answer."

Norman thought to himself, they must be at the temple for the wedding ceremony.

"Can we take the food up to the party room?" said Norman.

"What party room? We don't have any party room."

Norman took a twenty dollar bill out of his pocket and handed it to the tall gentleman. The man just stared and blinked. Norman replaced it with a fifty and held it out for the man to see. The staring and blinking continued. Norman replaced the fifty with a hundred.

"Oh that party room," he said, stuffing the cash into his shirt pocket. "You have to use the elevator in the back of the building. Good luck." Norman and his caravan drove around the building to a closed gate. Norman picked up the telephone at the gate.

"Open the gate so I can make my delivery."

The tall gentleman answered. "I can't leave my post now."

"Are you nuts?"

"That's the rules here and I never disobey the rules."

"I have another one of those bills in my hand," said Norman.

Five minutes passed and the good-looking, six-foot, two-hundred-pound man arrived and opened the gate. Norman shoved a hundred-dollar bill into his top pocket and headed to the elevator whereupon he was told that the elevator was not working. Norman shoved another hundred-dollar bill into the man's pocket, cursing Sam from Second Avenue Deli. The elevator lit up, and Norman and his crew proceeded to the party room and delivered the contents of the catering trucks. Norman thought to himself, no wonder Sam didn't want anything to do with this job.

The whole catering crew was in good spirits as they set up the party. It turned out to be the most fun party Norman had ever done. Everyone loved the crew, who mingled with the guests as much as they could get away with. Norman and his staff had a ball, made good money, and did a wedding that no one had ever done.

Back in the store the next day, the phone rang, "This is the Second Avenue Deli, is Norm there?"

"Hey Norm, pick up the phone!"

"This is Sam; I am having eight people over the house, how about catering the party?"

"No thanks, Sam."

"After I gave you that wonderful party?"

"Sam, thank you for the party. If anyone but Nelson's would have done that party, it would have bombed, but because of Nelson's experience and willingness to take chances, the party was a huge success. Thank you. By the way, you owe me three hundred dollars."

THE HAT-CHECK GIRLS*
By Elaine Nelson

How many times do you get to go to a Halloween wedding reception? Well, my friend Edie and I did. We drove into New York City around five o'clock on a Saturday night; the party was scheduled to begin at seven at North East Drive, an exclusive building in midtown Manhattan. The doorman had one of the parking boys take my car. We were very excited, all the more so when we saw the penthouse apartment where the affair was going to be held. Alas, we were not guests, but nevertheless we had an important job to do. We were the hatcheck girls. Neither one of us had ever done this before, but we assumed it would be fairly simple. It was the end of October, and the weather had turned cold. Coat racks had been ordered, but only one was delivered. We would have to make do.

We had a few stacks of receipt tickets to give to the guests as they handed us their heavy coats. One of the waiters came into our room and brought us whiskey sours. We drank the sours and were beginning to relax, and then the guests started to arrive. For fifteen minutes we checked coats, but the coat rack was already getting full. We had another round of whiskey sours. The next group of guests arrived with their coats and hats. It looked like we didn't have enough receipts, so we just tossed the hats and coats on the rack. We hoped we could figure it out later.

One particular couple came in with their noses in the air, snubbing us. By this time, Edie and I were feeling no pain because we had been drinking more whiskey sours. The husband handed me his navy-blue cashmere coat and snootily stated that we were not to put it near his wife's long fox coat. Guess where we put his coat? We were feeling great, enjoying an evening full of laughter and having fun with the guests. Suddenly Edie stopped laughing and looked at me. "How are we going to get these people their coats back?"

We had no tickets for the hats, so we just threw them on top of the rack and prayed we would find them when the time came to give them back. Between being buried in the coats and hats and trying to read the tickets, we couldn't see each other. I still can't figure out to this day how we did it. All the customers got their coats and hats back. Everyone was nice and left us tips, which we donated to animal rescue. It was great fun, but I think I will pass on the next party and just go back to being a mom to my three sons.

"Thank you Elaine and Edie for being so much fun and adding a special quality to this affair. There will never be another wedding like it. No one will forget it, and no one will forget the hatcheck girls who added to the fun!"—Your husband and friend, Norman.

CHICKEN

Morris was behind the counter when in walked Mila. Morris's eyes lit up; he had trouble with her before. He looked at the top of the counter where the chicken and other foods sat and thought about getting the chicken off the counter. Too late—she had a chicken in her hands and tried to hide it in her shopping bag.

"Hey put that chicken back, Mila!"

"What chicken? You crazy man???"

"The chicken you got in your shopping bag!" said Morris

"What shopping bag? I ain't got no shopping bag."

"What the hell is that big yellow bag you are holding?"

"I am taking my dirty laundry to the cleaners."

"You give me back my chicken! You are not getting away with it this time," said Morris.

"You touch my bag, Jew boy, and I will punch your fucking lights out and send you to the hospital!" said Mila.

"If you don't put my chicken back I will call the police and have you arrested."

"Listen to me Jew boy; if you call the police, I'll fucking destroy the place with you in it." Everyone at the bar was enjoying the excitement. They loved every minute of it. The fight went on.

"Wait a minute," Mila said. She walked over to the bar, handed the bag to one of the patrons, and told her if she did anything to the bag she would kill her. She said she was walking outside to get a piece of wood lying in the street, so she could put a hole in Morris's head. Out she went. Morris went to the door and watched as Mila picked up a piece of wood and started to run toward the door. Just as Mila got to the door, Morris closed it, and Mila ran into the door, causing blood to spurt from her nose.

She started to scream. "That Jew bastard hit me! Look, I'm bleeding!"

People stopped outside. "Somebody call an ambulance, this woman is hurt!" The crowd grew in size. Mila kept screaming that they ganged up on her, beat her up, and threw her out of the store. "Those Jew bastards, they stole my money and ripped my dress!"

The crowd continued to grow, "Get the Jew bastard!" they screamed.

A siren was heard in the distance; an ambulance was on its way. When it arrived, two medics got out. By this time, Mila was lying flat on the ground screaming of the pain she was in from the beating she had taken from Morris.

The crowd grew louder. "Look what those bastards have done to her."

The medics went back to the ambulance and brought out a stretcher. They went over to Mila. "Can you move?"

"No I can't move," she said. "I'm practically dying!"

"We are going to put you on a stretcher and take you to Columbia Medical emergency room for treatment. "

"Mila looked up. "What do you mean you are going to put me in a stretcher; you ain't going to put me in no stretcher. If you put your dirty, filthy, fucked-up hands on me, I will knock the shit out of you!"

"Lady, we are only trying to help you!" As the medic bent over Mila, she made a fist and knocked the medic on his ass. His nose was bleeding. She looked up at the crowd and said, "You saw it! He tried to rape me! You saw that bastard try to violate me!"

A voice came out of the crowd. "Lady, you are nuts."

A police car arrived. "Hey, what's going on here?" asked an officer.

"She is crazy; she's nuts," the crowd explained. The police officers went into Nelson's to hear the story for themselves. When they came back out they hauled Mila, screaming, into the police car for inciting a riot. They took her to the police station where she had been many times before. They put her in the hospital ward to clean her up, and because they could get no witness to the crime, they had to let her go.

After telling all the police to go fuck themselves, Mila left. A rough day, thought Morris as he started to close up the store. He looked out the front window, which was large and gave him a great view of the now empty and quiet street. He watched as a form in the distance grew larger and larger. It was a large woman in a dress carrying a big yellow bag in one hand and a brick in the other. As she got closer, Morris recognized Mila just as she threw a brick through the window, which sent shattered glass all over the floor. Mila then turned and headed toward the 169th Street subway. A police siren could be heard in the distance.

Morris called the insurance company, who then called the glass company, who sent out a truck with enough plywood to cover the window until the glass could be put in. The phone rang. Morris picked it up.

"Mr. Nelson, we have Mila here, we think she is the one who put the brick through your window. If you want to press charges you have to come down to the station right now and fill out papers."

"What do you think, Detective Goldberg?" said Morris.

"Do you have insurance, Mr. Nelson?"

"No."

"Do you have the time to spend in court when this case goes to trial?"

"No."

"Do you want to spend all night filling out papers?" said Goldberg.

"No."

"By the way Mr. Nelson, did you know that Mila is one of the head nurses of the Psychiatric Ward in Columbia?"

"No."

"Although we think she was high on drugs today, she has a decent reputation."

"Well that's a shock. I think she needs psychiatric help herself," said Morris.

"Well that's true but when a judge hears her story, he won't be tough on her."

"Goldberg, I'm going home. It's been a rough day."

"I hope I didn't say anything to change your mind," said Goldberg.

"No, nothing. Goldberg, why don't you drop by tomorrow, and I'll make you a nice corned-beef sandwich."

"Make it pastrami and you've got a deal."

HARLEM

Elias walked into Nelson's and asked for an outgoing pint of fresh homemade mushroom garlic soup,. Out of his pocket he pulled a roll of bills with a rubber band around it. He gave Millie the waitress a fifty-dollar bill and told her to keep the change. He put the wad of bills back into his pocket and walked outside to a beautiful white Cadillac. He got into the back of the car, and it drove away.

So it was that Norman first met Elias, a six-foot-tall, two-hundred-fifty-pound black man with a penchant for soup from Nelson's Restaurant. The next time Norman saw Elias was when he and his friends came in for lunch. Millie the waitress fell over herself to get to his table. He and his friends ordered the best Delmonico steaks with French fries and the best bottle of scotch in the house, a twenty-five-year-old black. For dessert they had homemade fruit strudel with coffee. "Who the hell sells fancy steaks in a kosher deli?" Morris ran out the door and went to the butcher shop where he picked up three Delmonico steaks.

After they had eaten, Elias looked at the check, which was two hundred dollars. He took out his wad of bills, took off the rubber band, and counted out three hundred-dollar bills. He handed them to the waitress, and he and his friends walked out to the sidewalk where the beautiful white Caddy picked them up. Millie the waitress nearly fainted. She had never seen a tip like that before. For as long as Millie worked at Nelson's, no other waitress could get within ten feet of Elias.

One day soon afterward, the phone rang. It was Elias. He was throwing a party for some of his friends that evening. Could Nelson's bring sandwiches and salads with paper goods to his bar in Harlem that evening? He expected about a hundred people to show. "Make sure we have plenty of food, around midnight would be great."

Morris and Norman loaded the jeep with platters of sandwiches and set out for Elias's bar. As they drove through Harlem, they saw people on the streets, and stores were open and still doing business. There were busy bars on every corner. Say what you will, but Harlem was a vibrant, very alive community.

As they got to Elias's bar, they saw crowds of people on the street outside. This was their territory; they were all black. Being the only whites, the men from Nelson's stood out like a sore thumb.

"Hey, what the hell you doin' here, you honkey? What makes you think you can come to our town? Get lost you bastards. You get out of your car and we'll send you to the fucking graveyard." It didn't look good. Elias finally arrived in his white caddy, stepped out and shouted to the crowd. You would have thought it was the Red Sea as the crowd parted and Elias made his way toward Nelson's delivery truck.

"Hey man, thanks for bringing the food; follow me to the bar," said Elias. Again the crowd parted as we brought the food to the bar. Elias kept throwing the white envelopes into the crowd. He turned to Morris and Norman and said, "Thank you, man." He then looked at the bartender and said, "Give these guys whatever they want."

"What I want," said Morris, "is to get the hell out of here."

"Follow me to your truck."

The sea parted once more as Morris and Norman got into the truck. Elias said he would see us back at the store tomorrow and pay the bill.

"Ok, let's get out of here." Morris maneuvered the truck around the crowd and headed back to Nelson's. He wasn't sure if Elias would show up to pay his bill, but at this moment he didn't give a damn; he was just happy to get the hell out of there. The next day when Morris opened the store a white Caddy was parked outside. Three well-dressed black men walked into Nelson's.

"How much, Morris?"

"Three hundred dollars." They took a wad of bills out of their pocket, placed the money on the counter and walked out. When Morris counted the money there were five one-hundred-dollar bills.

Morris hadn't seen Elias for a month. The phone rang. Florrie, Morris's wife was at the register. Morris picked up the phone; on the other end was Elias.

"Send a platter of sandwiches to my office, OK?"

"What's the address?"

Elias gave Morris the address and thanked him. "Hey Norman," Morris said to his son, "I got a delivery for you. Do me a favor and handle it, OK?" Norman loaded the platter into the truck and headed out to make the delivery. The address was a two-story brownstone house. No one seemed to be around. Norman unloaded the truck and started for the front door. A voice on a speaker said, "Identify yourself!"

"Nelson's Deli making a delivery for Elias."

"Come on in." Norman entered and walked into the front room. No one was there; on the table were stacks of money piled all over the place. Singles, fives, tens, and hundreds.

"Put the food on the empty table in the corner," a voice said. Norman didn't see anyone, just heard a voice. "How much?" it said.

"Two hundred."

"Help yourself to two fifty. And get lost."

"Thanks."

On another day at Nelson's, the phone rang with Elias again on the other end. "Let me speak to Morris or Norman."

"This is Norman."

"Norman, I am opening a night club and I want you to cater the opening night. I will supply all the help and dishes; all I need from you is the food, OK buddy? I'm opening tomorrow night. Be there around midnight; here is the address. OK, see you."

The next night around eleven, Norman loaded the truck with his helper and started out for Harlem. When Norman got to the address Elias had given him, he looked at the neighborhood. This couldn't be the right address. It was a block-long stretch of condemned and burnt-down houses on both sides of the street. As Norman looked down the street, he noticed that on each end of the block cars were parked as if to block off the entrances to the street. One was a white Caddy; the other was a Mercedes. Norman drove around the block and ended up in front of the white Caddy. The guys in the car called over the phone to tell Elias that Nelson's was here with the food.

"It's the house with the gray stairs." Just then, four or five taxis arrived and were waived through. Norman and his helper entered the house. Inside was a beautiful room set up with a bar, waiters dressed in tuxedos, a five-piece jazz band, tables, chairs, a dance floor, beautiful flowers, and a staircase decorated with fluffy clouds. There was a sign that said the Cloud Room.

As Norman delivered the food, more people kept arriving. They were beautifully dressed, some in tuxedos, some in gowns. The waiters met them at the door and offered them champagne cocktails. A beautiful woman dressed in a gorgeous gown with diamonds on her hands and in her hair greeted the guests.

"Elias was here earlier and left a message that he would stop at the store tomorrow. By the way, would you like to visit the Cloud Room?"

"No thank you," Norman said. He set up the food and headed out the door. The Caddy moved to let him depart.

The next day Elias arrived early in his white car. "Hey Norman it was great! Thanks! How much?"

LUNCHTIME

The bar had a good crowd that day. Many superintendents from the building adjacent to the store, post office delivery guys, produce delivery guys, and cops, who in those days, walked the beat and knew everyone. Of course they only drank ginger ale, wink, wink. For some lost souls, the bar was their home: working students from Columbia Med and doctors who usually took their drinks at the table. The way it worked, you sat at the bar, and the bartender poured you a drink, and then another, and then a third. You put your money on the bar, and half went to the register; half was the tip. Bartenders made big tips, and all the seats were taken. It cooled down around noon when the bar started to clear out. Five or six patrons were still at the bar discussing the upcoming bike race at the 168th Street Armory, which because of its size, has the largest bike racing track in the city and therefore has the biggest money bike race in New York.

Through the door walked a lean and mean-looking guy dressed in a typical bike racer outfit. He had a number on his t-shirt, tight shorts, bike racer shoes and a French beret on his head. He headed for the bar. The guys at the bar, most of whom own their own trucks or businesses, sized him up. This guy looked like one of the bike racers who come to town for the big bike race at the Armory. Frenchie sat down at the bar and with a slight accent, asked the bartender for a double scotch on the rocks. As his drink was being poured, he turned to the guys sitting at the bar and inquired about a bike race he had heard of taking place at the 168th Street Armory. Tommy Schlitz, a man weighing around three hundred pounds and six foot of muscle, walked over to Frenchie and patted him on the back. "Why the interest in the race?" he asked.

"I am a bike racer." Hearing this, the rest of the guys moved over and started to ask him questions.

"You French?"

"Yes."

"Where do you race in France?"

"I have raced all over Europe."

"What the hell are you doing here?"

Frenchie was jilted by his girlfriend who left him for another bike racer. He decided rather than kill her and her lover, he would come to America and make a new life for himself. He had been racing his entire life throughout Europe and France." Maybe you have read stories. I was in all the major races in Europe, and some even said I was the fastest bike racer they ever saw."

Max told the bartender to refill Frenchie's glass. As Frenchie sipped his drink he went on with his story. He arrived in New York a week ago. He took his luggage and his beautiful, classic, European Deluxe 495 bike with special wheels to the hotel in the Bowery where he rented a room. That night he went out to dinner. When he returned to his room, everything except for a box with his medals and newspaper articles was gone. The bastards had also stolen all the cash he thought would be safe under his mattress. Except for some money he had on him, everything was gone.

Tommy stood up at the bar and said, "Those sons a bitches! Those fucking bastards!" That being said the bartender poured Frenchie a double on the rocks, this time on the house. The guys at the bar invited Frenchie to stay for lunch. Frenchie wanted to leave; he was very depressed after telling his story. When Frankie put his big arms around Frenchie and led him to a table, Frenchie decided to stay. They had pastrami and corned beef sandwiches with a bottle of beer and continued to discuss the upcoming bike race. After lunch they all disbanded and set off in their different directions with the promise that they would all meet the next day in the afternoon at Nelson's Bar. As they left, Wally said, "My God that is a quality bike racer if I have ever seen one!"

The next day, all the same group was at the bar waiting for Frenchie to arrive. They had been talking about the bike race and had arrived at the same conclusion. If this guy was on the level—and they would test him first—they would all put in about $500 to get him settled and into shape; the race was coming up in one week. They had six days to get him ready. If he won the $50,000 purse, they would take out their expenses and split up the rest. Hernandez, the superintendent of three buildings in the area, came up with an idea. He would let Frenchie live in an abandoned apartment so he could keep an eye on him and make sure he was working out. As they were discussing the race, Frenchie walked up to the bar. Under his arm he had a box.

"Hello," he said and placed the box on the bar. The bartender poured him his usual. Little Sammy opened the conversation by asking, "What the hell is in the box?"

Whereupon Frenchie answered in no uncertain terms. "My fucking life, that's all; just my fucking life."

"Well then open the fucking box, and let's have a look."

Frenchie's eyes teared up, "You can look at what's in the box, but do not touch because it is the last things that are left in my life. If I did not have them to comfort me I would die."

"Yeah, yeah, yeah, open the box. We ain't going to touch anything, OK?"

Frenchie opened the box. Inside were medals in gold and in silver, with beautiful ribbons. The medals were inscribed in French. Lying next to them were dozens of newspaper articles from the French press.

Frenchie picked up a medal and began to read. "First Place in the French DeGuard Bike Race, 1980 given to Paul Croissant." There were different medals that all said pretty much the same thing. As Frenchie went on to read the articles, what they heard were heart wrenching stories about all the tough races in the rain and fog that Frenchie had won.

"What a guy! God bless him! How lucky we are that he found his way to us." The guys were all ecstatic. Everybody wanted to get a piece of the action. The more they talked about Frenchie, the more worked up everyone at the bar got. The guys got together and decided that they would not allow anyone else to get in on this deal. It was theirs and theirs alone. If this guy was what he said he was—and the medals and newspaper articles looked like proof for all to see—there could be many other races, and they could all make a lot of money.

"Goddamn it, there is no end to the possibilities!"

They called their friend Bernie for his advice. "How the hell do we test this guy?" For the last four days they had him doing leg exercises, and he did them all with grade-A marks. They fed him only the best steaks served with only the best wines. He looked good and ready. Bernie advised them of a friend that dealt in racing bikes. He could get them a deal. Bikes ran up to $5,000. But Bernie could get them a 20 percent discount. The bike was handmade with a new alloy, known for its lightness and speed. The boys added more cash to the pot—$500 more apiece.

Max was designated to pick up the bike. Little Sammy was told to pick up a stopwatch for timing. Everyone was excited for the next day. Around two o'clock when the traffic was a little slower would be a perfect time for the bike to be tested. Frenchie showed up in his new bike outfit. The boys had picked blue, white and red for their colors. Frenchie looked good; he had used his $250 allowance well. He got a massage, a haircut, and bought a new pair of sunglasses. He was looking sharp.

The boys decided they would make their bike a surprise. Everyone was there to watch Frenchie get his new bike. Frenchie was brought into the store and in the back stood this beautiful new bike, specially painted blue, white, and red to match his bike suit. Frenchie looked at the bike, tears coming to his eyes. He started to bawl like a baby. He hugged and kissed everyone and got down on his knees and thanked God for his new friends. "A round of drinks for everyone!" shouted the bartender. "God, the tips are good here!" he said.

Outside, the crowd from Nelson's gathered. They all begged for a piece of the action and once again they were turned away, but out of friendship for Frenchie, they all stayed to see him race. Two of the guys held up a ribbon from one side of the street to the other. The cop on the beat held back traffic as Frenchie mounted his beautiful new bike. Frankie stepped up, checked the stopwatch, and signaled Frenchie, Frenchie took off and went through the ribbon, and in what seemed like seconds, he was down the road and out of sight.

Frankie watched as the stopwatch spun its merry way around the dial. "What the hell is wrong with this stupid, stinking stopwatch. This fucking watch, it doesn't work!"

"What do you mean it doesn't work?"

"Frenchie should have been back here already!"

Five minutes passed, then ten, then fifteen, then a half hour, then an hour. Most of the crowd that was left burst out in hysterical laughter and left for the bar. The guys on the street soon left as well. Frankie stepped on the stopwatch and crushed it into little pieces. Max, Hernandez, Little Sammy, and Bernie headed for the bar. Frankie used every dirty word in the book and said that if he ever found that fucked-up little bastard, he would tear him limb from limb.

The deli was busy, the grills were busy, the bartenders were busy, the bar was crowded, and the bartenders could be heard saying "the tips are great!."

"TWENTY-FIVE MEN TURN TO THE STREETS OF MEMORY"*
Written by Paul L. Montgomery (originally appeared in the New York Times)

Yesterday morning in Washington Heights, under the surprised eyes of the residents, twenty-five joking, middle-aged men walked the streets of their youth talking of stickball and long summer evenings when the whole neighborhood was out on the stoops. "Most of these streets look different, but some things never change," said Dr. Edmund O. Rothchild, still remembered by his friends forty-six years later as the smallest and least athletic in the crowd. "My mother is still going to being hanging out the window of 170th St. yelling, 'Let my son play!'"

The outing, replete was Spaldeens and penny airplanes and noodle pudding at the last surviving delicatessen, was the idea of Sidney Reiner, the President of Cosmos Travel, who still has fond memories of the neighborhood in the days around World War II. "We were street kids," Mr. Reiner said of his friends, now doctors and lawyers, professionals and sales executives.

"There was no television, no air conditioning then; we were lower middle class with working parents. We played in the streets and yet it seemed like we never got in trouble. We have all seemed to do all right out in the world. I thought it would be fun for us to see each other again." Most of the participants came from the suburbs and some from Washington. "It's amazing," said Mr. Reiner, "I couldn't find one from Washington Heights."

The men, all of them around fifty, played basketball and stickball and punch ball and kidded each other about needing attention from several doctors present and talked about jokes that went over back in the 1940s.

For lunch there was pastrami and corned beef at Nelson's delicatessen at 170th Street and Broadway.

"CHOPPED LIVER SHALL RUNNETH OVER"*
Written by Rita Goldman (originally appeared in the New York Times

Being born and raised in upstate New York is in no way related to being born in New York City, I have always been told. They're a breed of their own. I never really knew what that meant, but this past week finally taught me. The neighbor guys all attended New York's PS 173. There was Jerry, Sid, Eddie, Paul, Alan, and Norman. We meet every day at the way, the J. Hood Right Park Wall in Washington Heights. We fought the Cobra's, the Fanwood's and the Beacon's attempts to plunder us, but mainly they scared the hell out of us. The guys really weren't fighters because they were too busy playing stickball from sewer to sewer and constantly rounding up a game of Johnny-kick-the-can or ringolevio.

The mothers hung the wash on the outside clotheslines. The guys not only survived but they became educated, first at different high schools, then at various colleges. So do all the guys make a decent living? Well, if college professors, lawyers, physicians, engineers, psychiatrists, sports editors, and top IRS men make a decent living, then the guys did succeed. Not a single guy went bad.

Early on June 4, the girls became cheerleaders while the now gray-haired men played basketball to the tune of their creaking joints and heaving chests. They were walking en masse to Nelson's Deli. Nelson's of course once a wall leaner has ordered up enough pastrami, corned beef, and roast beef to permanently disable a vegetarian. The schedule calls for a blanket party in Central Park prior to taking over the whole top floor of the elegant San Remo Restaurant.

HI HO, HI HO, IT'S OFF TO FLORIDA WE GO

My sister Sharon and her husband Barry lived in Florida for many years. Florrie, Morris's wife, went for a visit and fell in love with Florida. Florrie was convinced that it was time for Morris to retire, and without telling Morris, bought a condominium across from Sharon and Barry. The cost of the condo at that time was around $12,000. That was for a condo with a pool, a walkway around a beautiful lake, a giant meeting hall for parties, cards, movies, and other activities.

When the news got back to Nelson's, Al, Morris's brother and partner, who was desperate to get out of the deli business, decided he would also retire and Florida sounded great. The only problem with selling his share of Nelson's was that business was going down and the neighborhood was changing.

Al made the call to Norman, "Hey Norman, do you want to buy my share of Nelson's? I'm ready to retire." Norman loved the store in the neighborhood where he grew up, and without any knowledge of what the store was worth, he agreed to Al's price. He would be in partnership with Cousin Sidney. When Aunt Minnie heard the news, she decided she wanted to be in Florida with the rest of the family. Dora and Manny, my aunt and uncle, arrived in Florida and took a condo. Jerry Greenberg, Minnie's son, flew to Florida and took an apartment. All the apartments and the condos were close to each other.

Florrie looked out the window, which faced the pool. She saw most of the family sitting out at the pool and saw that Morris was in conversation with his brother Al. She hollered out the window, "Morris stop talking to Al." She had it in for Al; she felt he took advantage of Morris.

With Norman and Sidney putting in the time and using their experience to come up with new ideas, menu, and packaging, the store was becoming successful. The catering, restaurant, and bar business had picked up, and Nelson's was doing so well that Norman was able to double up on the notes to pay off Al. When Norman's share of the store was finally paid up, Al could not believe it.

He called up Norman. "Hey Norman, how come you stopped sending me money for the store?"

"Listen Al, check the notes, you will find you are paid in full."

Al replied, "How in the hell did you do that?"

The Salami Cutters were now getting used to Florida. They did the catering for the community. Florrie, their leader, who they loved and hated at the same time, looked out the window and hollered at Morris to get away from his brother Al.

When Elaine and Norman came to Florida to visit the family, a cooking war would start. As Norman and Elaine arrived, Minnie pulled them into her apartment. She had been cooking all week and was ready to impress Norman with her gourmet foods.

"Minnie, my mother will kill me if she finds out I ate your food," said Norman. Minnie, a large woman, blocked the door.

"Norman, just taste; your mother's food doesn't compare to my food." Norman and Elaine tried to get out the door, but Minnie blocked way. She said to Norman, "Eat and I will let you out." Norman and Elaine sat down at the table. The food was melt-in-your-mouth quality. There was a loud banging at the door.

"Are you in there Norman? That bitch better not be feeding you! If you stuff yourself with that garbage that she cooks, you won't be able to enjoy all your favorite foods I've made for you." The door flew open. Florrie grabbed her kids as if to free them from captivity. They followed her next door to her apartment where Morris was adding his personal touch to the food.

"Get away from my food, Morris. Go talk to your lousy brother while I feed the kids. Eat! Eat!"

"What eat? We ate at Minnie's," Norman said.

"Well Minnie's food is lousy. You couldn't have enjoyed what she served. My food is delicious, so eat!"

The door opened, and Dora arrived, holding strawberry shortcake on a tray and a homemade rugelach on another tray. "Are they ready for dessert yet?"

Norman and Elaine felt like they were being buried under a mountain of food. Florrie's eyes were on her son Norman to make sure he was eating. In his mind, Norman was floating out on a sea of food. As he stuffed his mouth he could feel himself drowning. He heard his mom say, "One more mouthful."

"One more mouthful of delicious food and you will have to carry me out of here on a stretcher," said Norman.

Florrie said to Dora, "He is so funny, comes up with such funny lines. I just love his sense of humor."

Dora cut her strawberry shortcake, flowing with fresh strawberries and fresh whipped cream. That night there was a big party at the pool - everybody brought big trays of food. It was delicious. Everyone sat around the pool rasping and farting.

Florrie eventually moved to a very pretty condo in another community. Norman thought it was spite, to keep Morris away from his brother. Minnie passed away, Dora passed away, Al and Mary left to be with their daughter in New York.

In later years, when Norman and Elaine went to Florida to visit, they found Jerry a delight to be with. He talked politics and told all kinds of stories. Florrie spent her last years in a home care hospital where Norman and Elaine went to visit her.

"Mom, how come when pop tried to talk to his brother you would scream and tell them not to talk?"

"What, me tell your father not to talk to his brother? I would never do that."

God bless them all; they are all gone now, but their memories live on.

All the money in the world could not make up for the good times and fun we had. They weren't for everybody, but for me they were the best family in the world.

ACKNOWLEDGEMENTS

I would like to thank my wife Elaine and my three sons Steven, Robert and Donny, for their never-ending support, review time and story contributions. A special thanks to Donny for encouraging me write this book, and for finding and managing all the great resources who helped to put this book together. I would also like to thank Kathleen Moore, for her patience and great efforts in helping me with the dictation of this book – there is no way I could have typed or edited this myself, and Kathleen did a tremendous job patiently listening to me and faithfully recording all of my crazy stories.

I would like to acknowledge and thank all the dedicated and wonderful people I have partnered and worked with over the years at Nelson's. Memories of Sidney, Bridie, Irene, Ibby, Tommy, Ralph, Frank, Juan, Bernie, Charley, Hector, and others will always be fond and fun memories – the store simply would not have worked without you.

Last, I want to send a big thank you to all of our customers who made Nelson's their destination for some of the best food in New York. I hope everyone enjoyed the high quality products we produced, and I am truly grateful to have served you.

ABOUT THE AUTHOR

Norman Nelson was born in New York City in the 1930s, and learned all about delicatessens while growing up in the family deli business. Norman attended Long Island University and served in the army during the Korean War. Upon receiving an honorable discharge, he joined Nelson's as his father's partner. Norman has three grown children, five grandchildren, and currently lives in retirement with his wife in sunny Florida. In addition to a lifetime of catering, woodworking and sculpture, Norman recently decided to take up writing. This is his first book.

Made in the USA
Columbia, SC
31 December 2017